ROBICHEAUX'S ROOTS

ROBICHEAUX'S ROOTS

CULTURE AND TRADITION IN
JAMES LEE BURKE'S
DAVE ROBICHEAUX NOVELS

PATRICIA M. GAITELY

Louisiana State University Press
Baton Rouge

Published by Louisiana State University Press
Copyright © 2016 by Louisiana State University Press
All rights reserved
Manufactured in the United States of America
LSU Press Paperback Original
First printing

Designer: Laura Roubique Gleason
Typeface: Minion Pro
Printer and binder: Maple Press

Material in chapter 4 first appeared in different form in "Perceptions and Misconceptions of Folk Belief in James Lee Burke's Dave Robicheaux Novels," *Louisiana Folklore Miscellany* 18 (2008): 91–108, and is reproduced with permission of the editor.

Material in chapters 5 and 6 first appeared in different form in "Robicheaux's Revenants: The Use and Function of the Revenant in James Lee Burke's Dave Robicheaux Novels," *Clues: A Journal of Detection* 28.2 (2010): 77–86; and as part of "'I Took No Joy in It': Southern Violence and Folk Justice in the Robicheaux Novels," from *A Violent Conscience: Essays on the Fiction of James Lee Burke*, © 2010, edited by Leonard Engel, both by permission of McFarland & Company, Inc., Box 611, Jefferson NC 28640.

Library of Congress Cataloging-in-Publication Data are available at the Library of Congress.

ISBN 978-0-8071-6416-7 (pbk.: alk. paper) — ISBN 978-0-8071-6417-4 (pdf) — ISBN 978-0-8071-6418-1 (epub) — ISBN 978-0-8071-6419-8 (mobi)

The paper in this book meets the guidelines for permanence and durability of the Committee on Production Guidelines for Book Longevity of the Council on Library Resources. ∞

In memory of my mother:
Brenda Mary Gaitely,
1932–1985

CONTENTS

Acknowledgments ix

Introduction: Putting Down Roots 1

1. Language, Dialect, and Folk Sayings 17
2. The Soundtrack of a Culture 35
3. Robicheaux's Roux 55
4. Beliefs along the Bayou 65
5. Something in the Water 77
6. Fighting the Good Fight: Folk Justice and Southern Violence 101
7. New Iberia: Dave Robicheaux's Hometown 113

Conclusion: The Roots Run Deep 133

Notes 137

Bibliography 141

Index 145

ACKNOWLEDGMENTS

First and foremost, my thanks go to the editorial staff at LSU Press who worked with me on this project, and who made it a very positive experience. In particular, my thanks go to acquisitions editor Margaret Lovecraft and copy editor Catherine Kadair. Their attention to detail and patience with a first-time author are very much appreciated, and I will always be grateful to them both. Several of my professors at the University of Louisiana–Lafayette encouraged my study of Burke's novels, and in particular I am grateful to Dr. Marcia Gaudet and Dr. Barry Jean Ancelet for the knowledge and insights on aspects of Louisiana culture that they shared with me. I would also like to thank my colleagues in the English Department at Middle Tennessee State University for their encouragement and support, as well as the FRCAC Committee, the College of Liberal Arts, and the College of Graduate Studies, all of which supported this project.

On a personal note, I want to thank my father, Lionel Gaitely, for his unwavering support and encouragement, and my uncle, Michael Finnis, a fellow Burke fan with whom I have had many enjoyable Robicheaux-related discussions. And I could not forget to mention my brother, Raymond Gaitely, who has always encouraged me in my endeavors. Of course, special thanks go to James Lee Burke because, obviously, without his creating such an enigmatic character in Dave Robicheaux, this book would not exist.

ROBICHEAUX'S ROOTS

INTRODUCTION

PUTTING DOWN ROOTS

In 1987, a novel entitled *The Neon Rain* was published. It was by a relatively unknown author, and it featured a detective by the name of Dave Robicheaux, a complex, flawed character who seemed to spend as much time struggling with his own inner demons as he did battling the criminals who frequented his decidedly sleazy New Orleans landscape, and whose endeavors often followed Robicheaux to the more idyllic New Iberia of his childhood. Robicheaux experienced conflict not only with his criminal foes, but also with departmental authority (indeed, any kind of authority) and its representatives. He understood the language of the criminal underworld, but he spoke as an educated man. His grasp of his own failings meant that, for Robicheaux, there was little black and white but many shades of gray.

The detective novel was far from being a new genre when James Lee Burke introduced Dave Robicheaux to readers. Neither was the concept of the flawed detective new. In fact, it might be argued that for many years the market had been flooded with such novels. What made Burke's debut novel featuring Robicheaux stand out from others of the genre was that Burke situated Robicheaux in a specific rural, ethnic culture and, after the first novel, in a peculiar and little-known locale. While most detective fiction is set in an urban environment, much of the action in Burke's novels takes place in rural southwestern Louisiana, specifically the town of New Iberia. Burke's protagonist is a Cajun with a Cajun name, an appetite for Cajun food, an appreciation for Cajun music, and roots that run deep in Cajun culture. Burke includes a smattering of what readers are to assume is Cajun French (but not enough to alienate those unfamiliar with the language) and introduces readers to people who claim to be *traiteurs,* or traditional healers who operate outside of the mainstream medical field. Robicheaux has a history of alcohol abuse and is a veteran of the Vietnam War, both of which attributes contribute to his internal conflicts and his empathy for other flawed individuals. Through such cultural attributes and other shaping factors, Burke creates a character who embodies a distinct culture. As a result, readers of his books come to appreciate, at least on some level, the Cajun culture that is such an important element of Robicheaux's background. For some readers, admittedly, the Cajun element can be problematic because of limited or misleading information. A reader in England to whom I introduced the Robicheaux novels told me that he thought Cajuns were a Native American tribe! Many of Burke's readers are more likely to be fans of detective fiction than of specifically Louisiana fiction, and more likely to be familiar with other writers of the genre than Louisiana authors such as Kate Chopin or Ernest Gaines. Additionally, much information dispersed via the media in the 1980s and 1990s about Cajun culture was biased and inaccurate, and inadequate in its ability to convey a true understanding of the Cajun people and their rich, complex culture.

Burke's creation of Robicheaux is at least partly responsible for my spending six years living in Lafayette, Louisiana. I first encountered Burke's novels while a student in Maryland. At the recommendation of a friend who knew my affinity for detective fiction with an edge, I began reading *Black Cherry Blues,* the third book in the series. While not immediately hooked, several novels later I was. Pursuing graduate studies in Tuscaloosa, Alabama, I began to visit Dave Robicheaux's Louisiana on a regular basis, both for research purposes and because I had begun to feel a growing affection for the place and the people. When selecting a place to study further, I changed majors in order to attend the University of Louisiana at Lafayette. Robicheaux is the reason I learned to eat crawfish and étouffée, and discovered the best places to hear live Cajun music and zydeco, both in tourist joints and those known only to the locals. In creating Dave Robicheaux, Burke provides his readers with not only a character, but a culture. It is this that defines Robicheaux as much as, if not more than, his experiences in Vietnam and his alcoholism. It is this aspect of the novels that provides a sense of place, and in effect the landscape and culture represented are as much a character in the books as anything or anyone else. Robicheaux and his cultural roots are inseparable; they are part and parcel of each other, and an appreciation and understanding of his culture enhances our enjoyment of the novels, allowing us to feel more involved in Robicheaux's activities and more connected with his experiences.

Burke uses cultural traditions to create this sense of place and to portray Cajun culture. Readers of Burke's novels find themselves fascinated by the place Robicheaux calls home, an area that is inherently southern (so that Burke's writing shares similarities with that of other distinctly southern writers) but that retains its own unique flavor. In fact, readers like me make what might be termed pilgrimages to Robicheaux's home area, so that the area has become, somewhat surprisingly, a destination for cultural tourism.

Of course, other writers of detective fiction have also situated their protagonists and their novels in a distinct environment. Although written a couple of decades before Burke began his series of novels, a couple of notable examples instantly recognizable to readers of the genre are Robert B. Parker's Spenser novels, which associate the detective with the city of Boston, and Tony Hillerman's Leaphorn novels, whose protagonist represents not merely a locale but also a culture, that of the Navajo. Readers familiar with Parker and Hillerman would probably agree that it would be difficult to imagine the stories being set elsewhere, or indeed "working" in an alternative locale. Both Parker and Hillerman employ the same strategy as Burke, but there are some differences, not based solely on choice of location. For Parker, the city of Boston is the central factor. Even though there is a culture associated with the city, it is the city itself that is important, complete with sports teams like the Red Sox, and local landmarks. For Hillerman, Leaphorn's connection is not so much to a specific location as it is to a tribal identity. His identity as a member of the Navajo tribe is what distinguishes him from other fictional detectives. In fact, upon first reading one of Hillerman's novels, I was uncertain as to which western state it was set in because the location was clearly secondary to the Navajo culture depicted. The name of the town is not important; what matters is that Leaphorn is a Navajo, and it could be argued that Leaphorn's identity is as much in not being "white" as it is in being Navajo. His connection to the land is certainly an important part of his identity but is secondary to other elements of the setting. Aspects of the tribal culture, sometimes compared to other tribal cultures and white culture, permeate the novels and have garnered Hillerman a considerable readership and interest in that culture, much as Burke's novels have.

Closer to Robicheaux's home, other authors have also set their detective novels in Louisiana. However, an aspect of Burke's Robicheaux novels that makes them distinct from other detective fiction set in Louisiana is the way that New Iberia, Robicheaux's hometown, is set apart from much of the rest of the state. This, in turn, makes his novels distinctive from other work with a Louisiana setting. Writers such as Julie Smith and Chris Wiltz also set their works in Louisiana, their best-known protagonists being Skip Langdon and Neal Rafferty, respectively. These novels, though, are set in New Orleans, a legendary place often associated with local traditions such as Mardi Gras. Such deeply rooted traditions are best understood by those inside the culture, but Mardi Gras has also become a media event, meaning that even those outside of the culture think they understand it and know what it is all about. Television shows from *Cops* to *NCIS: New Orleans* help to reinforce this impression. Even books by the aforementioned Smith, while not claiming to be "Cajun fiction," are presented for public consumption with such review comments as: "If you like your mysteries Cajun style, you may enjoy Julie Smith's Skip Langdon series" and "She catches the tricky nuances of Louisiana speech," as well as the ubiquitous "gumbo" review that seems to accompany almost any book with a Louisiana setting. Smith and Wiltz do include local references, such as Smith's description of the Easter parades in

Crescent City Kill, and her distinction between witchcraft and voodoo, one being described as New Age-y and unacceptable, and the latter "part of our heritage" (166). A clever reference in the same novel to the lack of storage in traditional New Orleans homes and, hence, the necessity for armoires, is an integral part of the story. Theirs are distinctly New Orleans stories, and the cultural details that are included are to establish this fact. Wiltz, in her series of novels featuring cop-turned-private detective Neal Rafferty, makes certain to distinguish between different neighborhoods of New Orleans and surrounding areas, such as Westwego, identifying nuanced characteristics that provide insights into the area that might not be appreciated by readers from elsewhere. The locale also lends itself nicely to detective fiction: a crime-ridden city coupled with an intriguing history and colorful blend of cultures. Burke, on the other hand, while setting portions of his Robicheaux stories in New Orleans, almost uses it as a foil for the true setting, and the place that has created Robicheaux: the small but historic town of New Iberia, fairly close in terms of geography to New Orleans but extreme in its cultural distinction. New Iberia is located in one of the twenty-two Louisiana parishes identified as Acadiana, and is commonly considered a Cajun town, while New Orleans is not and never has been Cajun, in spite of publicity materials and television shows that might suggest otherwise. Again, Burke has done what other authors have done, but he goes the extra mile (both literally and figuratively)!

New Iberia is an unlikely locale for what is often termed "hard-boiled" detective fiction, a fact that makes the contrast more striking and, arguably, appealing. Robicheaux's frequent forays into New Orleans and its crime-ridden streets provide a contrast between a city about which much has been written, and much of its cultural history marketed, and the town that he more closely associates with his formative years and experiences. Separated by about 150 miles, about a two-and-a-half hour drive either along Interstate 10 or through oil towns such as Morgan City, the two cities differ more than merely geographically. As the first novel, *The Neon Rain*, draws to a conclusion, a disillusioned Robicheaux turns in his badge to the New Orleans

Police Department and returns to the Louisiana of his boyhood, one of many attempts to regain the innocence of his past. Here, in New Iberia, Robicheaux hopes he will recover something that has been lost while living in New Orleans, little knowing that even this Eden has changed much as he has changed due to time, circumstances, and external forces. Much of Robicheaux's internal conflict stems from his fondness for the past and his dislike of change, especially change over which he has no control.

Burke portrays Robicheaux's past—his greatest influence—by the inclusion of what can be termed "cultural markers," things that draw the reader's attention to the Cajun culture being created as the backdrop for Robicheaux's life. New Iberia, in common with much of Louisiana, has a rich and unique legacy of tradition. Cajun music is still played at public events and festivals (and often over the radio and as a background for local advertisements); Cajun French is still spoken by the older generation at the barbershop, the local café, and the hardware store. Traditions and traditional beliefs still abound. Family ties remain strong, with members of different generations often living in close proximity to one another. Race relations are at once relaxed and strained. For Burke, and for Robicheaux, the past is never far away and rarely completely left behind, especially where unresolved issues are concerned. Ghosts, both physical reminders and metaphysical entities, make their presence felt. Secrets of the past are laid bare as floodwaters, a common feature of the landscape, unearth shallow graves, revealing their inhabitants and the truth that is often buried with them.

Although Burke was born in Texas, he spent much of his childhood in New Iberia, and as a young boy, he played along the banks of the Bayou Teche. He grew up knowing the local history and culture of his adopted hometown and passes these attributes along to Robicheaux, who also grew up close to the banks of the Teche. Burke's family roots go deep in New Iberia soil. One of the old houses on the town's Main Street belonged to his great-aunt, Roberta Burke, and Burke would visit there in the summer and learned to fish and swim where the backyard meets the Bayou Teche. His cousin Pierre Burke lived in the house across the bayou from the old Burke house. Both Burke and Robicheaux, as young boys, would find minié balls from the rifles of Confederate soldiers along the banks of the bayou. In Robicheaux's case, they are on the grounds of the home built by his father; in Burke's case, he found them on the grounds of his grandfather's/great-aunt's house. In light of his tangible connection with, and his knowledge of, the Civil War and its impact on his home state and hometown, Burke's Robicheaux is inclined to believe that what he first fears may be hallucinations, the appearance of Confederate soldiers and conversations with them, may in fact be real.

To bring to life the place and culture about which he writes, Burke delves into the distant and more recent past and incorporates actual events into his novels. Weather patterns from the Gulf of Mexico are recorded and built into the plots, so that Hurricanes Audrey and Katrina become literary as well as historical events. Floods associated with actual storms conceal and expose long-buried bones and secrets. A Nazi submarine, like those that patrolled the Gulf in the early 1940s, plays an integral role in *Dixie City Jam* as a modern-day Nazi tries to persuade a reluctant Robicheaux to locate and recover the vessel. The murder of a local teenage girl, which took place in the late 1990s, is a major part of the plot in *Jolie Blon's Bounce*. Events such as these, combined with Burke's knowledge and inclusion of local culture and tradition, contribute to the authenticity of the locale in the Robicheaux series. In fact, each time a new Robicheaux novel is published, residents of New Iberia wait to see who of local note will be included this time, and what area landmarks will be mentioned.

To further emphasize Robicheaux's links to southwest Louisiana's past, he is not only familiar with the popular music distinct to the area in the forties and fifties, but still owns and plays it. It is the soundtrack of his life and a tangible connection to his past. Such details make Burke's use of cultural tradition especially effective. Those who recognize the places mentioned in the novels, the characters he depicts, and the incidents to which he alludes speak to the authenticity of his writing. Those from outside the area feel as if they have a hometown guide who clues them in to the small details that bring the place to life.

Situating the novels in such a specific locale, Burke makes the town of New Iberia almost a character in itself. Although the first novel featuring Robicheaux is set almost exclusively in New Orleans, and Robicheaux often visits other locations such as Mississippi, Texas, and Montana (where Burke also has a residence), it is the town of New Iberia that readers identify most readily with the character. Dave Robicheaux and New Iberia are inextricably linked in the minds of readers. And, because of Robicheaux's memories of his boyhood home and the experiences he lived through there, the link becomes more tangible.

Whether deliberately or by chance, the publication of Burke's novels focusing on Louisiana's Cajun culture was timely. In the late 1980s, Cajun culture was being "discovered" by mainstream America in a variety of media. Paul Prudhomme was introducing Cajun food and cooking to a widespread audience; and the music group Beausoleil, under the leadership of master fiddle player and Louisiana native Michael Doucet, was beginning to receive national and international acclaim as they introduced the rest of the world to both traditional and progressive Cajun music.

Hollywood made its own attempts to cash in on the popularity of Cajun culture, generally depicting it in a less than flattering light in movies such as *Southern Comfort* (1981), *No Mercy* (1986), and *The Big Easy* (1987). None of these films made much of an effort to present a balanced or realistic picture of Cajun life in the late twentieth century; rather, they played on popularly held stereotypes of Cajuns as hard-drinking, fun-loving people who are hostile and sometimes outright homicidal toward outsiders, and infinitely more at home in the swamp than at the mall, more comfortable paddling through the bayou than driving down the interstate. It was not until the release of *Passion Fish* (1992) that a more balanced perspective began to be transmitted. In many of these movies, the emphasis is on Cajuns coming into contact, and conflict, with a culture other than their own—that of mainstream America in the 1980s and '90s. The impression given is that of a people living in the United States but with a distinctly different, and less advanced, culture. The movies emphasize the "foreignness" of Cajuns and their culture and do little to present a balanced perspective of Cajuns working in modern industry, attending college, and generally being part of mainstream American culture.

Similarly, in literature, the image of the Cajun has evolved over time. Kate Chopin, writing in the late nineteenth century, portrays many Cajun characters, most of whom confirm the image of the pastoral, somewhat unsophisticated Cajun whose worldview does not extend much beyond the bayou. A sense of geographic isolation tends to reinforce this image. Henry Wadsworth Longfellow's poem *Evangeline* probably introduced the Cajun to the literary world with greater success than any other writer of his time, but the impression is of people ruled and ultimately destroyed by passion. Over time, the image has changed somewhat as writers from within the culture have begun to self-represent.

More recently, writers such as Tim Gautreaux have offered a more multidimensional view of Cajun culture. Especially in his two collections of short stories, *Welding with Children* and *Same Place, Same Things,* the culture is presented through subtle details that would be easy for an outsider to miss or to react to simply with amusement, without appreciating the cultural markers that they actually represent. Some of the familiar attributes from earlier authors are still present, but so are motifs such as the strength and importance of family, the attachment to place, the significance of community, and (sometimes) the ability to adapt to a rapidly changing environment. Gautreaux writes at approximately the same time as Burke, and so the collision between late-twentieth-century mainstream America and the Louisiana Cajun culture is prominent in the writings of both authors. In Gautreaux's short stories, the observations are more subtle, in Burke's work, the tension between cultures is a defining aspect of Robicheaux's experiences. Dave is also an educated man, something often not seen in earlier literary depictions of Cajuns, and has a profession, albeit one that tends to keep him attached to his blue-collar roots. He is also a character with a conscience, a heart, and a slew of problems caused by his addiction to alcohol and exacerbated by his having served and been injured in the Vietnam War. For all his characteristics, both good and bad, he is a violent man who often operates outside of the bounds of the law, especially when he doubts the ability of the law and its representatives to resolve a situation to his satisfaction.

If the image of the Cajun in movies and most literature has tended to be less than flattering, it can be argued that Burke does not always challenge this. The impression in his novels, though, and especially in his creation of Dave Robicheaux, is not of a people maligned, but of a people who are complex and who are at once familiar to the reader and somewhat different, too. In utilizing some of the popularly held stereotypes, Burke relates to the assumptions some readers already have about Cajuns and offers a broader, more detailed, and also more nuanced and varied picture. Burke paints Robicheaux specifically as one who exhibits some of the best, and worst, of human qualities as well as what can be considered stereotypical Cajun characteristics. Robicheaux has many facets to his personality, a personality that, over the course of twenty books, has had plenty of time to develop and mature. This in itself might make Robicheaux a unique character in the annals of Cajun literature: a character who has matured before the reader's eyes. From the young former cop marrying Kansas girl Annie, to the man thrust into fatherhood upon finding and rescuing Alafair, to the man who loses one wife to murder, another to sickness, and who grows old along with a former nun, Robicheaux represents a changing Cajun culture and an evolving attitude toward the wider world and his own roots. Each experience has both deepened Robicheaux's roots and broadened his worldview.

Burke's inclusion of so many different cultural and traditional elements has made the reader privy to a very vivid picture of the life and culture of this unique segment of the United States. Foodways play an important part in the novels, as does music. Food and music are synonymous with celebration and with social gatherings in Louisiana, and Robicheaux is frequently a part of both. Burke depicts not only the types of foods usually associated with the area, but the settings in which they are served and the persons responsible for preparing them. These details can allude to both social class and cultural identity. In advertising, when "selling" Louisiana, food is often a part of the pack-

Introduction

age; when selling particular types of food, Louisiana culture is often part of the package. The two are inseparable, and Burke certainly feeds Robicheaux well with local fare. It is not by accident that Burke's characters have a tendency to consume boudin and crawfish rather than pizza and hamburgers. When Burke has Robicheaux and Annie attend a crawfish boil, be it at a political fundraiser or a music festival, he is using symbols associated by those outside the culture with the Cajun way of life. As with music, Burke manages to weave foodways into the plot, be it through a reference to a poor black woman who scars her hands shucking oysters for the more affluent to enjoy, or a reference to Robicheaux and his family going to Mulate's (a restaurant located in Breaux Bridge) to enjoy an evening of Cajun music.

Together with foodways, music can be an important indicator of cultural identity. Robicheaux listens not only to the Cajun fiddle and accordion music that he might have heard as a boy played in the neighborhood, at festivals, and on local radio, but also to swamp pop, blues, and zydeco, all types of music with strong links and origins in Louisiana's history. In this way, Burke emphasizes that southwest Louisiana is home to more than one ethnic or racial group, including Creole and other African American groups. He further uses the different musical genres to demonstrate how various ethnic and racial groups interact, or fail to interact, with one another.

For Robicheaux, it is through music above all else that he most strongly connects to his past. Each song is a conduit to an earlier time and a more innocent experience. In particular, "Jolie Blonde" seems to stir in Robicheaux a kind of bittersweet feeling for the past that he knows can never be regained. That song is associated in his mind not only with Cajun pride and an identification with that culture, but also with his own childhood and personal as well as cultural experiences.

Another area where the interplay of cultures is particularly nuanced in Burke's work is in his depiction of religion and of folk belief. Burke writes Robicheaux as a Catholic, and as someone skeptical of what he perceives as charlatanism, of those who would take advantage of the poor and disenfranchised in the name of religion. Robicheaux clearly finds comfort in his Catholic faith, even when it seems inadequate to answer his questions or solve his problems. However, there are other elements of belief that permeate the novels, some of which complement Robicheaux's Catholicism and some of which would appear to contradict its tenets. Local Louisiana traditions such as the *traiteur* (literally, "treater") are used to demonstrate the variety of coexisting belief systems, sometimes identified with specific social or ethnic groups and other times appearing more cross-cultural. Even more prevalent is the inclusion of what in folkloric terms might be called the *revenant,* the remaining or returning spirit of a deceased loved one or, in some cases, a deceased stranger. Often this figure inserts itself into Robicheaux's life at a time of crisis (of which there are many!) or at a time of intense personal loss. The revenant for Robicheaux can be someone with whom he has had an intensely intimate relationship, such as murdered wife Annie, or it can be someone of whom he has no recollection at all and whose life may not have intersected in real time with his own. Since our worldview is often strongly influenced by the culture around us, Robicheaux is not quick to dismiss such supernatural occurrences, even if they might appear to contradict the formal belief system to which he subscribes. It is interesting that the appearance of many of these supernatural figures occurs in an atmosphere of water, since this is such a strong element of the Louisiana landscape and also an important element of religious faith in terms of baptism and regeneration. This medium is often used as the means by which the dead can enter the presence of the living, and vice versa. Burke seems to empower this essential element for life as the meeting place for the living and the dead. Since Robicheaux lives by the water (and in one novel lives on a houseboat, literally *on* the water), and also inhabits a state where thundershowers routinely roll through on a typical summer afternoon, he is situated in a very expedient place in which to experience these visitations. Would the deserts of Nevada have provided such a fertile place for these experiences? Probably not.

One of the most obvious ways in which Burke provides a distinct locale for Robicheaux is through the use of language. Language is presented in a variety of ways reflecting the cultural diversity of the state. Sometimes French phrases are included, reflecting the French heritage

Introduction

of the area. Sometimes these phrases are interpreted within the text, sometimes not. When they are, the translation may or may not be literal. Sometimes it is implied. Dialect, a regional variation of formal or standard English, is also utilized by Burke, as are what might be termed "folk sayings" and anecdotes that have often been passed on to Robicheaux by his father (or by Batist) and that come to mind when confronted with a stressful or puzzling situation. These too serve the purpose of reinforcing the geographic and cultural location in that they often refer to local wildlife—alligators, armadillos, crawfish, and so on—as examples of how to respond to a given situation. The speech of each character denotes his or her cultural heritage, background, educational opportunities, and also, perhaps, place in the social hierarchy. The aforementioned Batist is a character with whom Robicheaux has had a longstanding relationship since Batist worked for his father. He is also an integral character in the novels, as much so as Robicheaux's friend and one-time partner, Cletus Purcel. Only once, in *Dixie City Jam*, is he identified by his full name, Batist Perry. Burke characterizes Batist's physical strength as second only to his loyalty to Robicheaux and his family. Robicheaux trusts him implicitly, not only because he is physically able to take care of himself but also because, although he is uneducated and also illiterate, Robicheaux recognizes in Batist a wisdom and innate ability to read a situation that belie his lack of sophistication and formal education. In *Dixie City Jam*, readers get a more detailed description of Batist:

> I had known him since I was a child, when he used to fur-trap with my father on Marsh Island. He couldn't read or write, not even his own name, and had difficulty recognizing numbers and dialing a telephone. He had never been outside the state of Louisiana, had voted for the first time in 1968, and knew nothing of national or world events. But he was one of the most honest and decent men I've known, and absolutely fearless and unflinching in an adversarial situation. (24)

Batist is African American, and although at times Robicheaux acknowledges the racial differences that exist between them, it is largely in the way he speaks that these differences are most apparent. Robicheaux understands Batist and his unorthodox sayings, whereas his

Kansas-born wife, Annie, is unable to do so. Robicheaux can also speak to the educated in their "language," but is familiar enough with the way his father talked to fit in with the less formally educated in his community. He is also literate in the language of the criminals with whom his job often forces him to associate, and it is this language that readers may find hardest to understand since their terminology is largely inaccessible to "outsiders" and less prone to literal interpretation.

Linguistically, Robicheaux reflects the changing demographics of the baby boomer generation, who have largely abandoned the French that their parents were not allowed to speak in schools and which is now spoken predominantly in immersion programs, by the elderly, and by those involved with the Cajun music scene. Efforts by groups such as CODOFIL (Council for the Development of French in Louisiana) have undoubtedly played a role in reviving the language, but it is not to these efforts that Burke writes. By interspersing standard English with the French language and the Cajun dialect in his novels, he reflects the actual speech of the people, many of whom seem unconcerned with preserving the language beyond the next generation.

Related to the use of language is the inclusion in the text of folk sayings, many of which are attributed to Robicheaux's father, Aldous, an oil-field worker with a limited education. The sayings mirror the language and dialect of the region; they are not generic in either style or substance. In referring to local wildlife, they both reinforce popular images within the region and emphasize the linguistic style of the region. The sayings also, of course, convey the importance of wisdom that does not come from a formal education or book learning but from experience, and passed on not in written form but by oral tradition.

With all the elements that Burke uses to create the cultural ambience that pervades his books, it is only to be expected that readers familiar with Burke's cultural signposts and who want to know more about Robicheaux's roots will come to associate certain details from the books with the place about which they read. Certainly, in the minds of readers, the town of New Iberia has taken on almost a life of its own. It is more than just another town in southwestern Louisiana;

it is Robicheaux's home, both as a boy and as an adult. Readers connect the town with the character, and many have made the journey to visit the hometown of their hero.

Burke is so accomplished at interweaving local tradition and culture in the detective novel genre that his readers want to experience the setting of his novels, rather than merely read about it. They want to eat at a crawfish boil and dance to a Cajun band at a fais-do-do. They too might encounter Confederate soldiers in the thick Louisiana mist following a thunderstorm! They want to experience the scenery that Burke describes with such relish and authentic detail, and which Robicheaux appreciates on such a poignant level. The New Iberia where Robicheaux lives is not without its problems, but it is still a small town where the residents know each other, most businesses are locally owned, and people have time to socialize with childhood friends and acquaintances in the park while listening to a band and buying a plate of crawfish to support a good cause. Burke's novels have brought widespread attention to the town, and even if visitors cannot visit Dave's Boat and Bait Business, they can, thanks to a local entrepreneur, buy a T-shirt saying that they were there. The Cajun culture that Burke portrays, and that Robicheaux embodies, is easily accessible.

In Dave Robicheaux, Burke has created a character that has captured the imaginations of readers worldwide. In Robicheaux, Burke can be said to have done what Beausoleil did for music lovers and what Paul Prudhomme did for food lovers: he has helped to promote an image of the culture of southwestern Louisiana, or "Cajun country," to a larger audience. His use of local culture and tradition gives the impression of "insider information," providing an intimate portrait of what many see as an exotic, different culture, one that they perceive as being somewhat removed from mainstream America in the twenty-first century. Mostly, though, what Robicheaux means to his readers is someone who would be on their side in a fight, who is fiercely loyal to family and friends, who understands his flaws and therefore tolerates them in others, who has a defined instinct with regard to right and wrong, and who is so anchored by his roots that it is hard sometimes for him to accept the world as it really is today. In other words, he is both Everyman and knight errant, a charming and irresistible combination!

What this book will do is to look in detail at some of the references that Burke uses as cultural touchstones and make them accessible to those less familiar with the culture. Burke's use of such details is often subtle, and it is easy for the casual reader, or for those who don't know a Cajun from a Creole,[1] to overlook them. Further explanation might both enhance the reading of the novels and help to explain aspects of Robicheaux's character that are difficult to understand. The importance of the land, the music, the language, the food, the family heritage, all play a part in making Robicheaux the fascinating, appealing character that his readers find him to be.

1
LANGUAGE, DIALECT, AND FOLK SAYINGS

One aspect of Burke's writing that clearly denotes a sense of place and of cultural context is his use of language and dialect, as well as folk sayings that might be heard in Dave Robicheaux's Louisiana. This aspect of the culture is one that clearly links Robicheaux to his family roots and his cultural heritage. It can be somewhat confusing, though, for those unfamiliar with the history of the Cajun people and their historic connection with the French culture. Although the daily use of French as a first language is rare in twenty-first-century Louisiana, speaking the language can still be one way to distinguish the insider from the outsider in the Cajun community. By having his characters speak occasionally in Cajun and Creole French and by including culturally relevant proverbs and folk sayings or colloquialisms, Burke takes a stereotypical characteristic of Cajuns and makes a statement that effectively distinguishes them from the average modern-day American, and sometimes from each other. Just as Tony Hillerman might include a Navajo term or saying in his novels, and comment on the ability or lack thereof of outsiders to understand the tribal language, Burke uses culturally relevant terms and sayings to denote a culture associated with Louisiana.

Folk speech is a term most commonly used to describe nonstandard language and dialect, but can also refer to folk sayings, colloquialisms, parables, and even folktales. Often, these aspects of speech identify who belongs to a group or culture (an "insider") and who is excluded (an "outsider"). Folk speech also tends to reflect the traditions, both oral and otherwise, and the values of a group of people. Burke incorporates not just the French language—which is still spoken in southwestern Louisiana, especially by older residents—but also different dialects and unusual ways of imparting advice and wisdom, particularly from one generation to another.

Although sparsely used throughout the novels, enough French and other dialect is included to create an impression of a place where standard English is not the only linguistic option. Many places have a local dialect that might confuse or mislead outsiders. In fact, any group of people who have something in common—what might be considered a "folk group"—tends to have a language or jargon that they use among themselves and that would need explaining to those outside the group. This might include the pronunciation of local place names, the identity of local landmarks, and shared cultural terms. In his Leaphorn novels, Hillerman makes occasional use of the Navajo language. The fact that Father Ingles, a white Catholic priest, "had mastered its complex tonalities so thoroughly that he could practice the Navajo pastime of spinning off puns and absurdities by pretending to slightly mispronounce his verbs" (*Dancehall of the Dead* 138) marks him as an outsider who has attempted to assimilate into the culture and can be somewhat trusted. In Burke's case, the occasional use of Cajun French denotes a place with strong ties to its European past and where old traditions, including those appreciated and held onto by Robicheaux, are still valued. In fact, the use of Cajun French may say as much about Robicheaux's unwillingness to let go of the past and to accept and acknowledge change as it does about the culture as a whole. It is similar to the use of language and dialect by regionalist author Kate Chopin in the late nineteenth century to allude to the variety of cultural and ethnic groups that inhabited, and continue to inhabit, Louisiana. Her short story "In Sabine" has three main male characters, each representing a different culture: Bud Aiken is the abusive Texan (distinct because he is not from Louisiana); Gregoire Santien is Creole (of French descent); and Uncle Mortimer is African American. The dialect of each helps the reader to identify which cultural group he represents. In addition, the only female character in the story, 'Tit Reine ("little queen"), is identified as Cajun. Aiken, the outsider, is written as lazy, ignorant, and unable to pronounce either the name Santien or even his own wife's name; he insists on calling her "Rain" (Chopin 34). So the use of dialect to identify the different groups prevalent in Louisiana is clearly not a new strategy.

Chopin also sprinkles her short stories with Creole French, as demonstrated in "La Belle Zoraïde." A young Creole servant finds herself reminded of an "old, half-forgotten Creole romance" (87) and begins to sing to herself the following:

> Lisett' to kité la plaine,
> Mo perdi bonhair à moué;
> Ziés à moué semblé fontaine,
> Dépi mo pa miré toué.
>
> (87)

According to the maid, the song is "a lover's lament for the loss of his mistress" (87), but the French used here is not standard or Parisian French, rather a Creole patois. As with Burke, Chopin uses such narrative details to indicate the variety of languages and dialects that make up the linguistic scene in late nineteenth-century Louisiana. Explicit reference to different types of French in Burke's novels occurs in *Sunset Limited*, when Batist, Robicheaux's employee and longtime friend, warns Robicheaux about a man looking for Robicheaux's old partner, Clete Purcel. As Batist describes the man, he says that he "started talking French" (285). Robicheaux asks, "What kind of French did he speak?" (285) because this information will help in his identification of the offender. Batist's response is: "I didn't t'ink about it. It didn't sound no different from us" (285), suggesting that Batist and Dave communicate so effectively and clearly with each other that such distinctions become irrelevant.

In Burke's novels, along with Cajun French (similar to Parisian French but with stronger links to the historical use of the language, much as Appalachian terms often have more in common with older forms of English) comes some Creole French, as spoken by Batist. Batist is black, representative of the Creole community as it exists in modern-day south Louisiana, and there are differences between Creole and Cajun French. One of the limited examples of Batist speaking French occurs in *Heaven's Prisoners,* when Batist assures Robicheaux that the men who murdered his wife are long gone by stating, "*C'est pas bon. Ils sont pa'tis*" (128). More often, the differences between Batist's dialect and Robicheaux's are demonstrated by exchanges in English between the two. Both Batist and Clarise (another longstanding employee of the Robicheauxs and Alafair's babysitter after Annie's death) speak a type of nonstandard English based on French sentence structure that seems to fascinate Robicheaux, no matter how familiar he has become with it over the years. When Clarise attempts to discipline the three-legged raccoon, Tripod, that is a part of the Robicheaux household and Robicheaux objects, she says of Tripod, "Ax him what he done, him" (*Black Cherry Blues* 8). Tripod's "crime" is that he has defecated in the basket full of clean laundry! As Alafair learns English, Dave comments that she is attending Catholic school but "seemed to learn more English from Clarise and Batist and his wife than she did from me and the nuns" (8). He continues: "A few lines you might hear from those three on any particular day: 'What time it is?' 'For how come you burn them leafs under my window, you?' 'While I was driving your truck, me, somebody pass a nail under the wheel and give it a big flat'" (8). Clearly Robicheaux both understands what is being said and is entertained by the colorful and graphic way in which these ideas are expressed. And although he wants Alafair to learn standard English and be aware of the "correct" way to speak, he does not seem particularly disturbed that at times she emulates Batist's way of talking. In one exception in *Black Cherry Blues,* he takes her to Montana and, aware that her background might make it hard for her to be accepted by her new classmates, comments: "Alafair, try not to talk like Batist. He's a good man, but he never went to school" (120).

But even if Burke's use of French in the novels is limited, speaking French has traditionally been one way in which Cajuns have set themselves apart from the rest of the United States. In the past, it was more out of necessity, or from lack of alternatives, that French remained the commonly spoken tongue in southwest Louisiana. Before Interstate 10 connected Acadiana with the rest of the state and with neighboring states, access to the region was limited and communication with other areas was often not essential. Neither was there any pressure to speak English—a factor that changed after World War II, when interaction with the rest of the states, and assimilation into mainstream American culture, became more commonplace. In the years following the war, there was more pressure to learn English in order to secure a place in the wider world. Schools began to frown upon children speaking French, then to actively punish it, until English took over as the dominant language. The outcome was to effectively eradicate the use of a language with which Cajuns commonly identified themselves, leading to a tendency to separate themselves from other aspects of their culture, including traditional music. Between the 1940s and the 1970s, this was the dominant shift. However, in homes and between generations, French was still spoken, especially to tell stories. This served several purposes: it allowed the teller of the story to be more fluent in the language in which he or she told a familiar tale, and it allowed the storyteller to isolate the audience for whom the story was intended.[1] In addition, French acts as an important "identity marker" that serves to underscore the origins and cultural allegiance of those telling the stories.

When Burke includes the occasional French phrase or dialect in a conversation between characters, sometimes he translates it. This allows the "outsider" reader access into Robicheaux's world. In the first of the Robicheaux novels, *The Neon Rain,* in which cultural roots are being established, Robicheaux is investigating the drowning of a black teenage girl from a poor background. Burke depicts the girl's parents as speaking with a dialect that identifies them as uneducated and unsophisticated. The girl's father, Mr. Deshotels, tells Robicheaux: "She gone off to New Orleans. I tolt her a colored girl from the country dint have no business there, her. She only a country girl. What she gonna do with them kind of people they got in New Orleans? I tell her that, me" (30). Burke not only writes the dialect phonetically, as Robicheaux would hear it, but he also adds the words "her" and "me" to the end of sentences, a linguistic device still used among Cajuns and

Creoles in south Louisiana, and one that reflects the original French sentence structure. Deshotels continues: "We had eleven, us. She the baby. I call her *tite cush-cush* cause she always love *cush-cush* when she a little girl. He'p me walk out front, you" (30). Again, the dialect identifies these as ordinary people, the kind of people that Robicheaux often encounters, ordinary people whose lives have been touched by extraordinary violence. Deshotels' reference to cush-cush is interesting in that it refers to a cornmeal-based dish often served for breakfast and one that used to be a staple in both the Creole and Cajun cultures. It can also be written as "couche-couche." Deshotels' character is representative of the Creole community, but Burke makes little distinction between Cajun and Creole dialects; he is, after all, writing a detective novel and not a linguistics manual! To most readers, the distinction would be unnecessary and possibly distracting.

Batist often uses a mixture of French and English with a strong dialectic flavor. In a scene from *Heaven's Prisoners,* Robicheaux ponders the fact that Annie, his new wife who is from Kansas, often cannot understand what Batist is saying. He recalls a time when Batist said to her, "*Mais,* t'row them t'ree cow over the fence some hay, you" (35). He begins that sentence with the French word *mais* (which means "but" in this context is more affirmative than anything else) and continues the rest of the sentence in dialect, with "you" tagged on the end. The dialect sounds authentic and helps to create the overall picture of Batist, a man who has rarely traveled far from his home and has not had the benefit of much education, while also giving an example of the kind of dialect Robicheaux has grown up around.

Conversation between Robicheaux and Batist is likewise often a mixture of French and English, an example of which is provided when Robicheaux tells Batist to watch out for a couple of men in a Corvette while he is gone. Batist asks, "*Qui c'est une Corvette,* Dave?" and Robicheaux answers in English, "It's a sports car, a white one," to which Batist responds, "What they do, them?" (35). The conversation switches smoothly from Louisiana French (Batist) to standard English (Robicheaux) to Louisiana dialect (Batist), without either man indicating it was unusual that a conversation should take place in such a man-

Language, Dialect, and Folk Sayings

ner. Indeed, this kind of exchange is not that unusual in southwestern Louisiana, especially among those who grew up in the region prior to World War II. As a visitor to Louisiana, I remember waking up one morning and hearing the elderly woman with whom I was staying carrying on a phone conversation in French. As I entered the room, she greeted me in English without a pause, then continued her phone conversation in French. This is a technique that Burke adeptly uses with some frequency that certainly resonates with those familiar with the culture.

There are times, however, when Batist and Robicheaux do have trouble communicating, in spite of a lifetime of practice. At one point, Robicheaux says of a conversation with Batist, "When I told him that the black man named Toot was possibly a *tonton macoute* from Haiti who practiced black magic, Batist got him confused with the *loup-garou*, the bayou equivalent of the lamia or werewolf, and was convinced that we should see a *traiteur* in order to find this *loup-garou* and fill his mouth and nostrils with dirt from a witch's grave" (*Heaven's Prisoners* 57). Not only is there miscommunication and misunderstanding regarding the terms *tonton macoute,* a henchman or political enforcer from Haiti (another French-speaking nation), and *loup-garou,* a legendary werewolf figure; amidst all this there is superstition and local custom and legend regarding the *traiteur* and possible effects of the *loup-garou* being on the loose, a possibility that is not without some merit in Batist's view. The miscommunication stems from Batist's not understanding the term that Robicheaux uses, coupled with different worldviews and cultural traditions. Therefore, Batist replaces a term with which he is unfamiliar with one that he can grasp, one that reflects his own cultural and linguistic expectations. Most of us learn language from our parents, our peers, and our community. Then, in school, what we have learned is often adjusted to some degree of standardization. Batist's limited schooling means that his frame of reference is still very much his own experience with his family and peers, and it is to this that he turns when unfamiliar terms are presented.

Unlike Batist, Robicheaux has received a formal education. Robicheaux is usually able to express himself in terms Batist can understand, and vice versa; he can "code switch," that is, go back and forth between two or more different forms of language or dialect.[2] Batist, on the other hand, can only speak in the manner that he learned from his parents and his community, even though he is depicted as an intelligent man who often has significant insights into situations that Robicheaux has overlooked. *Heaven's Prisoners* includes another meaningful exchange between the two that takes place in the moments following Annie's murder. Batist tries to convince Robicheaux that his wife's killers are long gone. When Robicheaux suggests cutting them off, Batist slips into French, saying *"C'est pas bon. Ils sont pa'tis"* (128), meaning, "It's no good. They're gone." Robicheaux suggests that they take the truck, and Batist shakes his head no. Batist's French words here are never translated, but the context makes it clear that he is trying to convince his friend that there is nothing they can do. The exclusive use of French not only makes the scene between the two men deeply intimate, basically excluding the reader, but also indicates that in a moment of crisis, Batist slips back into the language with which he is most familiar and can most readily express himself.

There is one other instance in the same novel where Burke chooses not to give a translation of the words he uses. When Robicheaux and his nemesis, Bubba Rocque, get into a fight, Robicheaux asks the defeated Rocque if he wants to go to the hospital. His response is *"Brasse ma chu,* Dave" (193), spelled phonetically. Robicheaux responds, "You going to cuss me because you lost a fight?" which implies but does not spell out the meaning. Rocque's words translate as "Kiss my ass," but the reader unacquainted with the language would not necessarily understand this, even though they might get the gist of the expression. This is one instance where Burke obviously does not see the need for the words to be literally understood by the "outsider"; the implication is sufficient to make the point.

On occasion, Burke has Robicheaux explain the unusual sentence structure that can result from using English words in a French pattern. In *Cadillac Jukebox,* Robicheaux asks Batist to identify a man, and Batist describes the man as "A guy puts earrings" (45). Robicheaux explains, "As was Batist's way, he translated French literally into English, in this case using the word *put* for *wear*" (45). Not only are the words literally translated, but the order of the words reflects their translation from sentence structures that are different from those in standard English.

When talking with Batist, an older person who is of the same generation as his father, Robicheaux frequently uses French because this is the language with which someone of that generation from that location would be most familiar and comfortable. When talking with someone from another place (Annie, for example), someone of his own generation, or someone who would not know or understand French, he generally uses standard English.

As the Robicheaux novels progress, and Robicheaux's identity as the "Cajun detective" has been established, Burke includes less French, and this perhaps also reflects the region's battle to preserve the language. At best, Burke's inclusion of French is sporadic. He uses it to establish the background and culture in which Robicheaux is rooted. Rarely can it be said to hinder the reader's understanding of the books; the gangster language and slang associated with the detective genre and New Orleans mob scene might provide more of a linguistic barrier for readers than the smattering of French that serves to contrast the rapidly vanishing rural, idyllic way of life with a lifestyle that reflects the trappings and culture of modern, mainstream America, a culture that Robicheaux seems to disdain. In fact, the case can be made that much of the truly important information conveyed in the novels is conveyed in nonstandard English, perhaps reinforcing Robicheaux's dislike for what has been lost by assimilation into the larger, lackluster culture.

It is significant that Burke uses French when Robicheaux's memories of his father, Aldous, put him in the role of storyteller, as he gives advice to his son from beyond the grave. Storytelling is one area where French has remained in common use in Louisiana, and Burke utilizes storytelling to emphasize the cultural distinction of the Cajuns. Rather than include whole stories (although this does happen on occasion), Burke tends to use snippets of "folk wisdom" passed on from father to son. Often these sayings occur to Robicheaux as he finds himself in a predicament for which there seems to be no answer, and they often come to mind as examples of things that his father taught him or that Batist tells him. Rarely do they come from those unconnected with his culture and his heritage.

In *The Neon Rain*, where Burke is establishing Robicheaux's character, Robicheaux recalls that his father "usually spoke to us in French, and he entertained us for years with an endless number of admonitions, observations, and folk stories that he said he'd learned from his father but that I think he made up as the situation demanded" (137). Robicheaux paraphrases in English some of his father's sayings as examples of the kind of things his father used to tell him, almost as an actor occasionally faces the camera and addresses the audience with personal information, stepping away from the script. These moments build a sense of connection and intimacy between Robicheaux and his readers. The sayings include, "Never do anything you don't want to, you" and "If everybody agrees upon it, it's got to be wrong" (137). Both of these sayings suggest a suspicion of majority and authority, an attitude that Robicheaux can be said to have inherited from his strongly independent father. He also states that his father firmly believed the crawfish, a product of Acadiana, would have been a more appropriate symbol of the United States than the eagle because, "If you put an eagle on a railroad track and a train comes along, what's that eagle going to do? He's going to fly, him. But you put a crawfish on that railroad track and what's he going to do? He's going to put up his claws to stop that train, him" (137).

Robicheaux also recalls a serious piece of advice that he can almost hear his father whisper to him from his watery grave in the Gulf: "When you've hunted through the whole marsh for the bull 'gator that ate your hog and you come up empty, go back where you started and commence again. You walked right over him" (137–38). As Robicheaux comments, "A cop had never been given a better suggestion" (138). Later in the same novel, as Robicheaux talks with his half-brother, Jimmie, who has been shot, he reminds him, "You remember what the old man used to say—'You pull on dat 'gator's tale, he gonna clean your kneecaps, him'" (312). This saying, reflecting the Cajun dialect of his father's time, is deeply rooted in Louisiana culture and uses its native wildlife as an example. In a time of crisis, it is an old familiar family saying that Robicheaux uses to reassure his brother, bringing to mind a time when their father helped them fight their battles. It is these thoughts that come to mind even after he has been to Vietnam, been to college, and earned a degree—suggesting that that their father is still helping Dave and Jimmie; his "folk wisdom" continues to influence and inform them as adults.

It is this wisdom that influences Robicheaux's behavior when, in the same novel, he later recalls, "My father used to say that an old armadillo is old because he's smart, and he doesn't leave his hole unless you give him an acceptable reason" (223). Once again, an animal familiar to the region and its inhabitants is featured, a creature to which the younger Robicheaux can easily relate. Burke also uses the weather as a basis for folk sayings. Robicheaux seems to have inherited his father's prediliction for this strategy, stating in *Heaven's Prisoners*: "Saints don't heed warnings because they consider them irrelevant. Fools don't heed them because they think the lightning dancing across the sky, the thunder rolling through the woods, are only there to enhance their lives in some mysterious way" (44). Two people have warned him that he is in danger; he sees a streak of lightning—a warning of an impending storm—cross the sky, yet he ignores these warnings. He relates another of his father's sayings to the sheriff, a man whom he likes but whose ability at law enforcement he doubts: "My father used to say that a catfish had whiskers so he'd never go into a hollow log he couldn't turn around in" (62). In this instance, Robicheaux is explaining his reticence to visit Immigration and Naturalization Services regarding a little girl whom he eventually adopts as his daughter. Once he has been to the agency, he may find himself in a situation from which it would be difficult to extricate himself. Or, to put it another way, Robicheaux considers it better to ask forgiveness than permission!

On another occasion, Robicheaux recalls a fishing trip during which he and his father become separated. Dave grows angry with his father and refuses to talk to him, and Aldous tells Dave that his anger is based on the fact that he was alone out there. He tells him, "Don't never do that, Dave, 'cause it's like that coon chewing off its own foot when he stick it in the trap" (*Heaven's Prisoners* 137). For Aldous, giving in to anger based on fear would be as harmful as a raccoon dismembering itself in order to free itself from a trap. On this occasion, Robicheaux does not heed the warning given by his father. He states, "A coon can chew through sinew and bone in a few minutes. I had a whole night to work on dismantling myself" (137). Robicheaux resorts to drink to numb the pain caused by the murder of his wife, Annie.

In a later novel, *Crusader's Cross*, Robicheaux shows the affection he had for his father, largely recalled in connection with the way he spoke: "My father, Big Aldous, spoke a form of English that was hardly a language. Once, when explaining to a neighbor the disappearance of the neighbor's troublesome hog, he said, 'I ain't meaned to hurt your pig, no, but I guess I probably did when my tractor wheel accidentally run over its head and broke its neck, and I had to eat it, me'" (207). He also explains that in the language he was more familiar with, French, Aldous was eloquent: "But when he spoke French he could translate his ideas in ways that were quite elevated. On the question of God's nature, he used to say, 'There are only two things you have to remember about Him: He has a sense of humor, and because He's a gentleman He always keeps His word'" (207). He acknowledges that his father might be deemed unsophisticated by the broader culture, but recognizes that he was able to express himself eloquently and powerfully in a way that both of them understood, even if it might not be fully appreciated by those outside the culture. His wisdom was not learned from books, but the hard way from experience and a deep familiarity with the environment and culture in which he was raised. Such wisdom attests to the adaptability and durability of the Cajun culture, attributes embodied in Aldous.

Robicheaux's other main source of folk wisdom is his friend Batist. Although he lacks a formal education and has spent his whole life in Louisiana, Batist has a fundamental understanding of the way things are and an instinct for when something is wrong. He also tends to put things into perspective, such as the time in *A Stained White*

Radiance when Robicheaux and his third wife, Bootsie, are discussing Bobby Earl, a character clearly based on Louisiana politician and one-time Klansman David Duke. Batist tells them, "That man Bobby Earl ain't been all bad," explaining, "*Mais* black folk wasn't votin' for a long time. Now they is. I bet you ain't t'ought about that, no" (282). As Batist points out, Earl's evil has had the unintended consequence of encouraging people to vote against him, a point that had been overlooked by Robicheaux. In a later novel, *Cadillac Jukebox,* Batist shares his wisdom with Dave again, this time using animals to make his point concerning a visitor to Robicheaux's bait shop to whom he takes a disliking. Batist says, "Dave, let me ax you somet'ing. You got to bring a 'gator in your hog lot to learn 'gators eat pigs?" (50). In both of these examples, Batist uses dialect; in the second, he transposes the letters "s" and "k" in "ask" so that it is pronounced "ax"—a common feature of Louisiana dialect among both black and white speakers. Batist stops short of saying outright that he dislikes the stranger, instead voicing his concerns in terms of a predatory animal and its prey. As often happens, Batist's instincts prove to be accurate; the visitor attacks Robicheaux as he calls for a police cruiser to pick the man up.

Throughout the novels, Batist demonstrates his connection to his own roots, which run at least as deep as Robicheaux's. It is unclear whether he believes some of the folklore and legends he has grown up with, but these are clearly a part of his culture and he accepts them as such. When he sees a red moon in *Purple Cane Road,* he listens to Robicheaux's explanation that it is caused by all the dust in the air stirred up by the wind, then responds, "Old people say back in slave days they poured hog blood in the ground under a moon like this" (103). When Robicheaux asks why this might be, he claims it is to "make the corn and cane bigger. Same reason people kill a gator and plant it in the field" (103). In this case, Batist perceives the red moon as some kind of warning concerning potential danger for Robicheaux's friend and former partner, Clete Purcel.

One way Burke uses this type of speech strategy is to express opinions that may not be easily accepted or considered politically correct. For example, *In the Electric Mist with Confederate Dead* contains a scene where Robicheaux is talking to an old man, Sam, who might have some information about a lynching that took place decades earlier. Sam is a product of his time and culture, but he does not want to say directly what he thinks about relationships between the races, so he cloaks his opinion in a folk expression. He tells Robicheaux, "A bluejay don't set on a mockin'bird's nest" (74), using two different species of birds to make the point that things that are different should not mix, nor mate, and implying that such a coupling would defy the natural order. After he has softened the blow of his racist views with his bird analogy, he continues, "The Lord made people a different color for a reason" (74). Interestingly, the same comparison about birds not mating outside of their species is used by some Native American groups who reject marriage outside of their tribe. This is especially relevant when the amount of Native blood can be used to determine the person's claim to a certain heritage, and when the allocation of lands can be based on such numbers.

When Burke uses a folk saying or tale passed on from generation to generation, it is usually to make a moral point or to issue advice on how to live. Research suggests that in a culture of slavery, slave tales passed on orally were used as survival strategies,[3] and much of Batist's wisdom indicates that it is his wits and understanding of his environment that have helped him to survive and avoid conflict in a racially divided society. Undoubtedly, most of his worldview has been passed on orally within his family from generation to generation, as when he explains the meaning and purpose of the red moon, crediting the saying to "some old people."

As the series of novels progresses, and Robicheaux ages, often lamenting the passing of the world in which he grew up, the inclusion of Cajun French and other examples of dialect seem also to lessen. Burke still uses them sporadically, but not with the frequency with which they appeared in the earlier novels. In *Pegasus Descending*, Robicheaux comments on a conversation with Mack Bertrand, adding, "It was no time for my lament on the problems of my generation and the lost innocence of a French-speaking culture that has become little more than a chimerical emanation of itself, packaged and sold to tourists" (274). However, it does not seem that the language he associates with his past has become any less important to Robicheaux, since in *Last Car to Elysian Fields*, he says to an adversary: "My father taught me to hunt, Mr. LeJeune. He used to say, 'Don't be shooting at nothin' you cain't see on the other side of, no.' He was a simple man, but I always admired his humanity and remembered his words," to which LeJeune responds, "As always, your second meaning eludes me" (328). And, as in earlier novels, Burke provides a nuanced view of ethnic groups in Louisiana with information such as the following to describe a group of "blue-collar mulattos whose race was hard to determine" (120): "They drifted back and forth across the color line, married into both white and black families, still spoke French among themselves, and tended to be conscious of manners and family traditions" (120). To accentuate the complexity of the racial distinctions in this culture, he continues to write Batist's diction in dialect and even uses a term that, outside of his own group, would be seen as an insult (in fact, its "in group" usage is still up for debate). As Batist tells Dave the story of Junior Crudup. the blues artist from Angola prison in *Last Car*, Batist concludes his story: "They put Junior Crudup on the Red Hat Gang. Every nigger in Lou'sana feared that name, Dave. The ones come off it wasn't never the same" (30). If Batist's use of the "n" word here seems casual and lacking in meaning, in *Burning Angel* it becomes obvious that Batist has chosen this word deliberately and endowed it with a particular meaning. At their boat-and-bait business, Batist asks Robicheaux, "You know why a nigger'd be setting in one of our boats this morning?" Robicheaux responds, "Batist, you need to forget that word," but Batist then emphasizes the word: "This is a *nigger* carry a razor and a gun. He ain't here to rent boats" (43). As Robicheaux, somewhat bewildered, asks him to "start over," Batist continues, "This is a nigger been in jail, carry a razor on a string round his neck" (43). To Batist, this man and he have nothing in common, and he feels entitled to call him by that loaded term in order to identify the kind of person he is rather than his race or color.

In a more recently published novel, *Creole Belle*, Cajun French is all but excluded, except for two small but significant incidents. Robicheaux lies in his hospital bed listening to Jolie Melton sing "La Jolie Blon" on his iPod, and describes the experience "as though she were speaking French to me from a bygone era, one that went all the way back to the time of Evangeline and the flight of the Acadian people from Nova Scotia to the bayou country of South Louisiana" (28). Having just been shot, Robicheaux is acutely aware of his own mortality and now associates the language not only with his immediate family and its history, but with that of his ancestors. Cajun French has taken on a broader and perhaps deeper meaning, even while it is used less often.

The language is again referenced in *Creole Belle* when Catin Segura, a female deputy who witnessed the death of her would-be rapist, Jesse LeBoeuf, confesses to Robicheaux, "I lied to you, Dave" (476). She continues, at his prompting, "I told you Jesse LeBoeuf said something when he was dying in my bathtub . . . I told you I didn't know what he said because I don't talk French" (477). In his confusion, Robicheaux assumes that she does, after all, speak French, but she corrects him: "No, not at all. But I wrote down what the words sounded like" (477). She has held back this information because she is afraid that LeBoeuf's last words might identify the shooter who saved her life. Clearly she sees his death as justifiable and does not feel that her savior should be punished for his actions. When asked what the words are, Catin reads them phonetically, "Jam, mon, tea, orange" (477). Robicheaux considers them: "She repeated them slowly. Though she had written down the words phonetically, if I was correct in my perception, they weren't far off the mark. The words Jesse had probably spoken were '*J'aime mon 'tit ange*'" (478), which he interprets as "I love my little angel." The words not only help Robicheaux with his case but also serve to demonstrate the way in which, over time, the use of Cajun French has become fragmented, despite valiant efforts to reintroduce it to the area and to support its use, especially among the younger generations, since the 1970s. It is also significant that, while Robicheaux's third wife, Bootsie Mouton, shares his heritage, his second and fourth wives do not and neither does his adopted daughter, Alafair. And although she is noted as "a descendent of French Huguenots" (*Black Cherry Blues* 252) and is from Martinique, not enough information is given about his first wife to make a determination.

Burke features dialect and folk sayings in his novels for two main reasons. First, they link Robicheaux with the past. Aldous may be deceased, but his influence on his son continues as Robicheaux remembers fondly the sayings that his father used to both entertain and educate. The tales he tells, the sayings he passes on, are his way of providing for his sons the information they need in order to survive in an environment that Aldous knows will not always be kind. Batist, having worked for Aldous, is more than merely an employee; he, too, is a link to the past and to Robicheaux's father. He also passes on wisdom in the best way he knows, not by the written word or by sending Robicheaux to college, but by explaining the world they both inhabit as he sees it. The influence of these two men on Robicheaux demonstrates the importance of the oral tradition in the Cajun culture.

Burke's second purpose in using these linguistic devices is to paint a fuller portrait of the area about which he writes. Once again, he relies on popular stereotypes. When Aldous talks about the crawfish being a better choice for a national symbol, a symbol of southwestern Louisiana is also brought into play. When Batist references an alligator, he is returning to an image that has become a mainstay of Burke's novels. The locale becomes an integral part of each story that Burke creates.

In Robicheaux, though, Burke creates a character who is not limited by his Cajun background, and it is noteworthy that the advice he passes on to his daughter, Alafair, seldom takes on the same attributes as that given him by his father. He is familiar with the stereotypes because he has both grown up with them and distanced himself from them, having experienced other cultures. He has also had the experience of being married to Annie, a cultural outsider (and, ironically, someone who did not survive in her new environment), who has helped him to see his own culture through the eyes of one to whom it is distinctly foreign.

The overall impact of these inclusions, be they colloquial or linguistic, is to add color and dimension to the culture about which Burke writes. They work as a complement to the foodways and music featured in the novels, as the language employed in the music is also used in everyday speech, and the animals that are so significant in local cuisine (like crawfish) turn up as characters in folk sayings. As Burke incorporates these different elements into his works, he adds layers to the picture he creates of a culture where each piece is significant and all the pieces interconnect; all play a role in molding Robicheaux.

2

THE SOUNDTRACK OF A CULTURE

Nothing else evokes a time and place in one's mind as powerfully as a song. Music can take us back to the precise moment we first heard a song, the season when the song was a hit, and the people we spent time with when the song was playing. For Robicheaux, music serves as a conduit to the past in a way that little else can. When he hears a song on the radio or the jukebox, or while driving across the Atchafalaya Basin, his response, more often than not, is to reminisce about a Louisiana that is long past, and that will never return. And when he hears *that* song, "La Jolie Blonde," a song so deeply rooted in Cajun culture that it is often referred to as the Cajun national anthem, the scene evoked is as fresh in his mind as the first time he heard it. Louisiana is somewhat unique in the United States in that local radio stations, especially in the southwestern part of the state, play songs by local artists whether they are popular in other parts of the country or not. This is especially true of artists playing Cajun music, such as Wayne Toups and Zydecajun (the band's name suggesting the blend of music types performed). The live music scene is alive and well, and local listeners want to hear on the radio the same bands that they hear at festivals and in the dance halls that permeate that part of the state. It is a way of acknowledging and celebrating local talent and the local culture, and in this regard Louisiana seems to be something of a delightful anomaly.

More than one type of music represents southwestern Louisiana, and likewise, more than one type of music appears in Burke's novels. Nor does all music have the same effect on Robicheaux; that with which he was most familiar growing up, and which represents his culture, has the greatest impact—namely, "traditional" Cajun music, as well as swamp pop. Blues and, to a lesser extent, zydeco also play essential roles in the novels, representing for Burke aspects of African American culture in south Louisiana. Zydeco is still largely claimed by African Americans; many of its white followers are from outside the culture and are either visitors or transplants. Blues and zydeco are used to help depict the broader, more diverse culture of the region but, especially in the case of zydeco, tend not to have such personal meaning for Robicheaux. In fact, zydeco, more often played in bars than at family events, is likely to be linked with his drinking days, a time he has no desire to revisit. Portrayed as carrying the most emotional impact for Robicheaux is Cajun music, which incorporates elements of traditional French music, black Creole and Native American influences, and traces of country and western, together with additions from other immigrant groups (such as Germans, who brought the accordion) (Ancelet).

When describing Cajun music, renowned Cajun musician and accordian maker Marc Savoy compares it to a "gumbo made of various ingredients and spices." According to Savoy, a sound is developed by starting with a basic melody, then adding syncopation and embellishments until "it starts to *taste* like a Cajun song" (Ancelet, Edwards, and Pitre 137). Burke's use of Cajun music does more than set a particular scene within a novel; it appeals to a multiplicity of senses as it provides a vital link between past and present. By including a variety of types of music indigenous to the area, Burke accentuates the different locales and ethnic and racial groups that inhabit his novels, and sometimes uses the music directly to suggest the tension and lack of understanding that this diversity can create.

Locally produced music permeates Burke's books, even inspiring some of the novel titles. *Black Cherry Blues* is named for a song written and performed by an ex-con featured in the work. *Cadillac Jukebox* refers to a top-of-the-line jukebox showcasing some of the most popular songs of the region from the 1950s and 1960s, the time when

Robicheaux was growing up. The "jam" in *Dixie City Jam* can refer either to the trouble that Robicheaux inevitably gets himself into or to a jam session common to jazz (and other) musicians in cities such as New Orleans. *Jolie Blon's Bounce* refers to an updated version of "La Jolie Blonde."

One of Robicheaux's defining characteristics is a preoccupation with the past. Often, Burke situates Robicheaux in a scene where a particular song is mentioned in order to emphasize Robicheaux's longing for a time gone by. In *Cadillac Jukebox,* Robicheaux has been given a replica of a 1950s Wurlitzer jukebox: "It sat squat and heavy in the corner, its plastic casing marbled with orange and red and purple light, the rows of 45 rpm records arrayed in a shiny black semicircle inside the viewing glass" (249). Robicheaux plays Jimmy Clanton's "Just a Dream," Harry Choates's recording of "La Jolie Blon," and Nathan Abshire's "Pine Grove Blues" (250). "Just a Dream" is a swamp pop hit of a kind popular in the 1950s in south Louisiana. The term *swamp pop* was coined to describe this locally grown music largely based on the New Orleans stylings of artists such as Fats Domino and distinguished by its triple note style. Shane Bernard describes swamp pop as "typified by highly emotional vocals, simple, unaffected (and occasionally bilingual) lyrics, tripleting honky-tonk pianos, bellowing sax sections, and a strong rhythm and blues backbeat" (5).[1] One wonders whether it could have been created anywhere other than in south Louisiana. As Robicheaux peruses the selections on the jukebox, he comments on the effect the songs have on him: "Their voices and music were out of another era, one that we thought would never end. But it did, incrementally, in ways that seemed inconsequential at the time, like the unexpected arrival at the front gate of a sun-browned oil lease man in khaki work clothes who seemed little different from the rest of us" (*Cadillac Jukebox* 250). The locally produced music evokes a time for Robicheaux when Acadiana was largely isolated from mainstream USA. But it was also a time of change, change that happened so gradually that no one was aware of how intense and pervasive it would be.

Later in the same novel, Robicheaux returns to the song "La Jolie

Blon," this time reflecting on the lives of two men who recorded it: "There were two recordings of 'La Jolie Blon' in the half-moon rack, one by Harry Choates and the other by Iry LeJeune. I had never thought about it before, but both men's lives seemed to be always associated with that haunting, beautiful song, one that was so pure in its sense of loss you didn't have to understand French to comprehend what the singer felt. 'La Jolie Blon' wasn't about a lost love. It was about the end of an era" (302–303). Robicheaux continues in thought: "Iry LeJeune was killed on the highway, changing a tire, and Harry Choates died in alcoholic madness in the Austin city jail, either after beating his head bloody against the bars or being beaten unmercifully by his jailers." He muses: "Maybe their tragic denouements had nothing to do with a song that had the power to break the heart. Maybe such a conclusion was a product of my own alcoholic mentality. But I had to grieve just a moment on their passing, just as I did for Jerry Joe, and maybe for all of us who tried to hold on to a time that was quickly passing away" (303).

The Jerry Joe whom Robicheaux refers to is Jerry Joe Plumb, the childhood friend who gave the jukebox to Robicheaux as a gift, perhaps partly to atone for stealing from Robicheaux as a child when he felt humiliated by his inadequacies. Robicheaux has these thoughts in the moments after he discovers that Jerry Joe has been beaten to death in New Orleans, while news of his death is still a raw wound in Robicheaux's psyche. As Robicheaux debates the past, and the memories that the song and its singers evoke, he concludes, "But you can't recover the past with a recording that's forty years old, nor revise all the moments when you might have made life a little better for the dead" (303–304). For Robicheaux, the song and the past are closely intertwined with feelings of regret, loss, and poignancy about a time that is at best bittersweet, no matter how much he might long for its return.

In *Black Cherry Blues,* Robicheaux refers to "La Jolie Blonde" briefly as "the song that always broke my heart" (175). In *Crusader's Cross,* it is "the song that will always remain for me the most haunting, unforgettable lament ever recorded" (158). It should be noted that the various spellings of the song's title reflect the variety of ways it has been written over the years. Not only do the song's lyrics often undergo change with each performance and each performer, so the spelling of its title reflects its fluidity, as if the song itself were a living thing subject to change, much as Robicheaux's memories of the past are, too, subject to interpretation.

In *Cadillac Jukebox*, Robicheaux hears his daughter Alafair, a Central American native, play "La Jolie Blonde" on her record player. It is as if, by playing the song that evokes such a strong and poignant response in her father, she is connecting herself to not only the person he is now, but his past and heritage also. As well as being legally bonded into his family, she has become culturally bonded to him.

In *Heaven's Prisoners*, Burke situates "La Jolie Blonde" in a scene about foodways of the area, confirming the fact that food and music go hand-in-hand in southwestern Louisiana. Robicheaux and Annie are attending a baseball game at the New Iberia park, and some firemen are having a crawfish boil in the open air pavilion. Robicheaux comments: "The trees were full of barbecue smoke, and you could smell the crawfish from the pavilion and the hot *boudin* that a Negro sold from a handcart. Then I heard a French string band play 'Jolie Blonde' in the pavilion, and I felt as though once again I were looking through a hole in the dimension at the south Louisiana in which I had grown up" (100). Robicheaux then utters the lyrics to himself in both French and English, although the English is not a direct translation of the French.

Jolie blonde, gardez donc c'est t'as fait.
Ta m'as quit-té pour t'en aller,
Pour t'en aller avec un autre que moi.

Jolie blonde, pretty girl,
Flower of my heart,
I'll love you forever
My jolie blonde.
(100)

Burke seems to have great affection for the song, and it warrants at least a mention in other novels as well. In *A Stained White Radiance*,

Robicheaux is talking on the telephone with Weldon Sonnier, who is in a pool hall. In the background, Robicheaux can hear "La Jolie Blonde" being played on the jukebox. The Sonnier family harks back to Dave's childhood and growing up in New Iberia, and the memories for Dave, while often idealized, are not always pleasant. The Sonnier family has secrets, including a father who may or may not be dead, child abuse, and filial incest. Just pages later, Robicheaux ruminates on the song and on his conversation with Sonnier: "Weldon had his problems, but I had mine, too," and continues: "Once again I felt like the outside world was having its way with us, that it had found something vulnerable or weak or perhaps even desirous in us that allowed the venal and the meretricious to leave us with less of ourselves, less of a way of life that had been as sweet in the mouth as peeled sugarcane, as poignant and heartbreaking in its passing as the words to 'La Jolie Blonde' on Tee Neg's jukebox" (204–205). That Burke uses this particular song so frequently to evoke such times in Robicheaux's life is notable. "La Jolie Blonde" is one of the most instantly recognizable Cajun songs, played by many of the Cajun bands that frequent Lafayette restaurants and bars, and undoubtedly one of the most requested by tourists.

As stated earlier, Burke does not limit himself to Cajun music when creating the ambience of the area he describes. In addition to its Cajun population, south Louisiana is also home to large numbers of black Creoles and other African Americans. Blues and zydeco play a part in representing African American culture in Burke's writing, and are also used to trace the tensions that have historically existed between different cultures. For example, Burke characterizes Lyle Sonnier, a character in *A Stained White Radiance*, as having played in a zydeco band. A picture of the band hangs in the home of Lyle's sister, Drew; as noted below the picture, the band is called the Catahoula Ramblers. There are two notable dichotomies here. First, while not unheard of, it is unusual for a white man such as Sonnier to front a zydeco band. It is not uncommon for Cajun bands to incorporate a few zydeco songs into their repertoires, but that Sonnier leads a zydeco band is rather remarkable. Sonnier goes on to become a televangelist, a medium that often exhibits a blend of preaching styles and crosses racial boundaries.

Second, perhaps ironically, the name of Sonnier's band calls to mind a Cajun band rather than a zydeco one. As a result of the process of the "Americanization" of southwestern Louisiana during the 1930s and 1940s, bands began to lose their distinctive sound and to adapt to different styles, especially that of western swing from Texas, its much larger neighboring state. Bands such as the Hackberry Ramblers played a mixture of traditional Cajun and bluegrass and country and western. The steel guitar was added, and lyrics began to switch from French to English.[2] A band whose name included such words as Ramblers, Playboys, or Aces would be presumed to be one of these Cajun bands incorporating different, but overwhelmingly white, styles of music. As someone grounded in the culture, Burke would understand this distinction. He deliberately mixes Cajun and zydeco elements here. Certainly, there are aspects of Cajun music that share common ground with zydeco. The two types of music have some of the same origins and influences while each has developed a distinct identity. For example, both Cajun music and zydeco tend to use the accordion, although the piano accordion is more common in zydeco, and the fiddle is usually absent in zydeco (Canray Fontenot being a notable exception). Zydeco tends to have a more syncopated rhythm and to be faster paced than Cajun music. Also, Cajun songs are often sung in French, while zydeco is now trending toward English. It can be said, though, that the two have developed along parallel lines, one distinction being the influence on zydeco of what is known as the juré, or Creole shout and ring dance tradition. In his article "Lomax in Louisiana: Trials and Triumph," Barry Jean Ancelet recalls first hearing the juré when listening to a collection of recordings by folklorist Alan Lomax. He quotes Lomax, who states that the style was widespread among Creole communities in western Louisiana, and refers to the juré as the "missing link" (6) in the development of zydeco, influencing both the musical style and the dance style associated with it. The juré was very rhythmic, accompanied by shouts and a repeated refrain, and participants danced around inside church "in a shuffling, body-shaking fashion" (6).

When Burke uses the term "Negro-Cajun music" to describe zydeco in *Black Cherry Blues,* Robicheaux is in a phone conversation with someone making his first visit to Cajun country and who is therefore unfamiliar with the local terminology and distinctions. For Robicheaux, it is not the focus of the conversation, so he tries to brush it off and move on to more important business. When Dan Nygurski, a DEA agent, describes a bar to Robicheaux as "a zydeco place or something like that," he then asks, "What is that anyway?" Robicheaux responds, "It's Negro-Cajun music. It means 'vegetables' all mixed up" (40), giving one explanation of the origin of the word *zydeco* (the French word for beans, *les haricots*).

In the rest of the Robicheaux novels, Burke more closely associates zydeco with the African American culture in which it has its roots. *A Morning for Flamingos* includes a scene at what is described as a "juke joint," where "a zydeco band with an accordion, washboard, thimbles, and an electric bass was setting up on a small stage surrounded by orange lights and chicken wire" (30). The rest of the paragraph conjures the atmosphere at the bar: "Behind the musicians a huge window fan sucked the cigarette smoke out into the rain, and their clothes fluttered in the breeze like bird's feathers. Two deep at the bar, the customers ate *boudin* and pickled hog's feet off paper plates, drank long-necked Jax and wine *spotioti,* a mixture of muscat and whiskey that can fry your head for a week" (30). Again, food and music are linked, but the scene varies considerably from the typical Cajun affair. This is not a public, family-oriented event held in the park or at a crawfish boil. This is a bar where the patrons are all adults, and the atmosphere is far from wholesome. For Robicheaux, this kind of place holds memories of a past he would like to escape rather than embrace, which helps explain why he does not convey the same affection for the music he associates with this setting. It is also in this setting that Robicheaux first encounters Gros Mama Goula, a woman described in terms that suggest a cross between a *traiteur* (a traditional French healer) and a voodoo practitioner.

In a later scene, Robicheaux returns to the juke joint, and as he pulls up, "through a big fan humming in the back wall I could hear the zydeco band pounding it out":

> *Mo mange bien, mo bois bon vin,*
> *Ça pas coute moi à rien*
> *Ma fille aime gumbo filé*
> *Mo l'aime ma fille aussie.*
>
> (35)

Marcia Gaudet translates these lyrics as follows:

> I eat well, I drink good wine
> And it costs me nothing
> My girl loves gumbo filé
> And it loves my girl also.

According to Gaudet, this is a version of a Creole and Cajun folk song entitled "Mo Cher Cousin," usually associated with black Creoles. Gaudet surmises that "it was probably a black folk song, originally sung by the cook in the kitchen of a wealthy family" (73).[3] So this Creole folk song, probably dating back to slave times, appears here as a zydeco song. It is still sung in French and has retained much of its original meaning, although the context has been lost over time.

It is significant that Burke does not choose to translate these lyrics, as if they have no personal meaning for Robicheaux. Certainly, he does not comment on them the way he does those of "La Jolie Blonde." Robicheaux revisits the bar scene in *In the Electric Mist with Confederate Dead*. There, he describes Red's Bar as located in a "dilapidated, racially mixed neighborhood of unsurfaced streets, stagnant rain ditches coated with mosquitoes, and vacant lots strewn with lawn trash and automobile parts" (194). Robicheaux speculates that the owner had probably intended the place to be a "low-bottom bar where you didn't have to make comparisons or where you could get laid and not worry about your own inadequacies" (195). But the bar had become a success, largely because the owner had hired black musicians to play there ("because they were cheap") and had inadvertently ended up with "one of the best new *zydeco* bands in southwestern Louisiana" (195). If zydeco does not affect Robicheaux the way Cajun music does, he still acknowledges the talent of the musicians and their impact on south Louisiana culture. As no band is playing that night, Robicheaux selects "Hey 'Tite Fille" on the jukebox, an old song by the recognized king of zydeco, Clifton Chenier.

It would be fair to say that Burke uses Cajun music and zydeco in different ways in his Robicheaux novels. For Robicheaux, Cajun music is an integral part of his past and evokes strong memories of events and scenes from his childhood. Zydeco, on the other hand, has a different bearing on his past and is less representative of his cultural history. It is more likely to be associated with the seedy underworld that he came to inhabit after his descent into alcoholism and with times he would rather put out of his mind than dwell upon fondly.

The styles of dance associated with Cajun music and zydeco also differ significantly, the two having developed in private versus public spaces and from different roots (although there is some overlap). While Cajun and zydeco waltzes are almost identical, the two-step is a different matter. In Cajun dance, the couple moves around the floor in a pattern that follows other dancers. In zydeco, the two-step is a dance where couples remain isolated from other couples, staying in the same place on the floor, and the moves have more in common with a rhythm and blues style of dance. This distinction can be traced back to the formation of the two styles of dance. Cajun dance, with its European roots, developed largely at private gatherings and balls held in people's homes and in which all generations participated (Brasseaux 163). These dances, known as fais-do-dos, were a way for people to socialize and celebrate at the end of a long week. The term *fais-do-do* translates as "go to sleep" and refers to the concept of a baby or small child being carried around the dance floor by a parent or grandparent, being lulled to sleep by the rhythm of the music as they are held close to the adult. Even today, when Cajun music is played in a public setting, it is common to see children dancing with older family members. So, the Cajun style of dance reflects the environment and family dynamic in which it developed. In contrast, the style of dance associated with zydeco exhibits African and Caribbean influences (Ancelet). European elements were incorporated into the waltz, but the two-step shows more influence from non-European cultures. Zydeco has developed in a more public setting and also tends to be danced to by adult couples rather than have intergenerational participants. This has affected the dynamic of moves being performed and the type of moves deemed appropriate.

It is really in *Jolie Blon's Bounce* that the two music traditions come together, but unfortunately not in a way that suggests a peaceable blend between the races or cultures. The incident is referred to by Robicheaux simply as a "moment of contrasts" (171), and the scene occurs at a gumbo cookoff in City Park, New Iberia. Robicheaux notes the azaleas in bloom, the shouts of the children, the live oaks, and the gaiety of the crowd on what he refers to as "the first day of a verdant and joyous summer" (170). It is against this backdrop that Tee Bobby Hulin, a talented musician and a suspect in the murder of a local teenaged girl, steps up and, in Robicheaux's words, "mounted a knocked-together stage with his band, plugged the jack of his electric guitar into the sound system, and went into a re-created version of 'Jolie Blon' I had never heard before" (172). Robicheaux refers to this zydeco rendition of a song that has deep personal meaning for him as "a perfect moment in music that probably had no specific origin or plan" (172).

After the remainder of Hulin's set, Robicheaux asks him about the song. Hulin replies that he has just written it, that he has not tried it on an audience before, and that "souped-up zydeco's hot in some clubs" in Los Angeles (172). Hulin could not have selected a song more closely associated with white Cajun culture than "Jolie Blon," and he has mixed it with elements of zydeco to concoct a new blend. He notes that it didn't seem to go down well with the audience. Robicheaux, though, appreciates the song and the progression that it demonstrates. However, tension is not far removed from the scene; in the next moment, the parents of the murdered girl, Amanda Boudreau, approach

Robicheaux. Boudreau was white; the man suspected of her murder is black. Mrs. Boudreau says of Hulin: "He's here, playing at a concert, and the man who supposedly represents our daughter chats with him by the beer stand. I can't quite express my feelings. You'll have to forgive me" (173). The encounter leads to "drunk dreams" for Robicheaux, who is never adequately equipped to deal with direct conflict. Ultimately, it is discovered that Hulin did indeed play a part in Boudreau's death.

According to Barry Ancelet, "there is an unmistakable tendency toward soul and rhythm & blues among Louisiana Creole musicians." Thus it is not surprising that blues music also plays an important role in Burke's novels, helping him flesh out the south Louisiana setting and culture in all their complexity. Burke frequently associates blues music with characters who have spent time in Angola, the state penitentiary. Blues is often understood as an individual expression of a communal experience, representing not only the story of the person singing the blues, but the experience of the African American community as well. In *Jolie Blon's Bounce,* Robicheaux mentions the jukebox given to him in *Cadillac Jukebox* and selects "The Things That I Used to Do," by Guitar Slim. He comments: "I had never heard a voice filled with as much sorrow as his. There was no self-pity in the song, only acceptance of the terrible conclusion that what he loved most in the world, his wife, had become profligate and had not only rejected his love but had given herself to an evil man" (39). Robicheaux adds that Guitar Slim was thirty-two when he died of alcoholism. There are obvious parallels to Dave's life: his mother left his father and abandoned the young Robicheaux, and Robicheaux also fought the battle with alcohol that Guitar Slim seemingly lost. Batist asks Robicheaux, "That's old-time blues, ain't it?" Robicheaux does not directly answer him but, as so often occurs, is taken back in his mind by the song:

> The lyrics and the bell-like reverberation of Guitar Slim's rolling chords haunted me. Without ever using words to describe either the locale or the era in which he had lived, his song re-created the Louisiana I had been raised in: the endless fields of sugarcane thrashing in the wind

under a darkening sky, yellow dirt roads and the Hadacol and Jax beer signs nailed on the sides of general stores, horse-drawn buggies that people tethered in stands of gum trees during Sunday Mass, clapboard juke joints where Gatemouth Brown and Smiley Lewis and Lloyd Price played, and the brothel districts that flourished from sunset to dawn and somehow became invisible in the morning light. (40)

It might be considered unusual that a person's reverie on the past would include references to a brothel when other details point to the innocence of the era, but the music, complete with its gut-wrenching acceptance of an imperfect life, brings out more in Robicheaux than just a memory of a perfect time. It allows that the past also included the unsavory and the unacknowledged. It is not so much the bittersweet poignancy of "Jolie Blon," even as that is a song of loss and lament, but a realistic acceptance of the past. The scene ends with news that Hulin has attempted to hang himself at the local jail.

While it is hardly surprising that the blues are linked with bad times, in *Purple Cane Road,* Burke has the music played by a man who has been physically as well as psychologically disfigured. Robicheaux visits with Bob Cale, a man whom he believes has been wrongly accused of a crime. He describes Cale thus: "He wore steel picks on the fingers of his right hand and the sawed-off, machine-buffed neck of a glass bottle on the index fingers of his left. He slid the bottle neck up and down the strings of the guitar and sang, 'I'm going where the water tastes like cherry wine, 'cause the Georgia water tastes like turpentine'" (254). Robicheaux adds that Cale's hand is withered, "the fingers crimped together like the dried paw of an animal" (255). Cale explains that he lived for fifteen years at Carville, the state hospital for those suffering from leprosy. Cale says, "That was back in the days when people like me was walled off from the rest of y'all" (255). His rendition of the blues is associated with sadness, misery, and alienation from mainstream society—surely valid reasons to sing the blues.

If ever a book lent itself to the blues, it must be Burke's *Black Cherry Blues,* which tells the story of Robicheaux attempting to cope with the death of his second wife, Annie, his "jolie blonde." In this book, it is a white man, Dixie Lee Pugh, Robicheaux's roommate from his freshman year at Southwestern Louisiana Institute in the mid-1950s, who sings, plays, and lives the blues. Robicheaux recalls that Pugh flunked out of college during his first semester, "then went to Memphis and cut two records at the same studio where Carl Perkins, Johnny Cash, and Elvis began their careers" (4). Pugh, whose life is clearly modeled on that of Jerry Lee Lewis, became a major recording star, and Robicheaux acknowledges that he has something going for him that many others of his ilk lacked: "He was the real article, an honest-to-God white blues singer. He learned his music in the Baptist church, but somebody in that little cotton and pecan-orchard town rubbed a lot of pain into him, too, because it was in everything he sang and it wasn't manufactured for the moment either" (4). Pugh may be white, but it is his disassociation from society that again marks him as an excellent purveyor of the blues. Robicheaux recounts some of the stories that followed in the wake of Pugh's fame, the "four or five failed marriages, the death of one of his children in a fire, a hit-and-run accident and DWI in Texas that put him in Huntsville pen" (4). According to Robicheaux, Pugh was a kid from a river town north of Baton Rouge, which brings to mind Ferriday, Lewis's hometown. Other incidents in the novel seem more reminiscent of scenes from the life of Roy Orbison, another Sun Studio recording artist.

Robicheaux occasionally listens to the blues, prompted by particular circumstances in his life. In *The Neon Rain*, he returns from Angola, where he has visited a man on death row who will be executed at midnight. The incident brings to mind lines he once heard sung by a black inmate at Angola:

> I ax my bossman, Bossman, tell me what's right.
> He whupped my left, said, Boy, now you know what's right.
> I wonder why they burn a man twelve o'clock hour at night.
> The current much stronger; the peoples turn out all the light.
>
> (8)

Another painful experience for Robicheaux prompts a dose of the blues. After visiting his half-brother, Jimmie, in the hospital after he has been shot, Robicheaux says, "I listened to an old recording of Blind Lemon Jefferson":

> Dig my grave with a silver spade
> And see that my grave is kept clean
> O dear Lord, lower me down on a golden chain.
>
> (246)

Robicheaux then ponders why "only black people seemed to treat death realistically in their art.... When Billie Holliday, Blind Lemon Jefferson, or Leadbelly sang about it, you heard the cock of the prison guard's rifle, saw the black silhouette suspended from a tree against a dying red sun, smelled the hot pine box being lowered into the same Mississippi soil a sharecropper had labored against all his life" (247). Robicheaux recognizes that death is treated realistically by those for whom it is an ever imminent possibility. Although his own life has not been free of tragedy, he does not explicitly connect his own experiences with the blues since it is, from his cultural perspective, a music expressing the experiences of the black community.

Robicheaux returns to the blues theme in *Last Car to Elysian Fields*, where character Junior Crudup is referred to as "the blues man," a musician who has associations with famous blues singer and Angola Prison inmate Leadbelly. When Crudup dies at Angola, Robicheaux gradually uncovers the story behind his death. He is lured into the investigation when Father Jimmie, the local Catholic priest, tells him: "Junior's daughter owns a twelve-string guitar she thinks might have belonged to Leadbelly. Maybe you could take a look at it" (9). When he examines the guitar, "The strings were gone, the tuning keys stiff with rust, the sound hole coated with cobweb. I turned the guitar on its belly and looked at three words that were scratched into the back of the neck: *Huddie Love Sarie*" (11). Robicheaux comments: "Leadbelly's real name was Huddie Ledbetter. His wife was named Sarie" (11). Leadbelly, of course, was a real, legendary blues musician while Crudup is fictional. Castille, too, is fictional, while John and Alan Lomax were actual folklorists. The seamless intermingling of fictional and historical characters increases the authenticity of the novel, and the world that the novel represents.

As the story unfolds, Robicheaux listens to "two ancient .78 recordings made by Junior Crudup in the 1940s. As with Leadbelly, the double-strung bass strings on his guitar were tuned an octave apart. . . . His voice was haunting. No, that's not the right word. It drifted above the notes like a moan" (17). He consults Batist, who knew Junior Crudup and who tells Robicheaux a story that he compares to "stories that are just too awful to hear, the kind that people press on you after A.A. meetings or in the late-hour bars, and that later you cannot rid yourself of" (27). According to Batist, in Junior's early teen years he played in a band whose black lead singer had "the most beautiful voice you ever heard" (30). One night, as they played at a white juke joint in Ville Platte, a white woman dancing to the music walked over and patted her handkerchief on the singer's sweating brow. The singer was later beaten savagely and run over by "five white men drunk on moonshine" (30), a scene witnessed by young Crudup, causing him to lose his trust in mankind. It is also a scene clearly based on the racially motivated beating of Creole musician Amédé Ardoin in the 1940s. Batist mentions that Crudup was later jailed for getting caught "sleeping wit' a white man's wife" (30). Robicheaux also learns that someone came to the penitentiary and made recordings of some of the convicts. At first he thinks it might have been John or Alan Lomax, father and son who collected folk and blues songs from, among others, Leadbelly, but he learns instead that it was a local man, Castille LeJeune.

After hearing Crudup's story, Robicheaux reflects: "Did you ever have a song in your mind that you couldn't get rid of? For me, at least on that Monday afternoon, it was 'Goodnight Irene.' I kept thinking of Junior Crudup sitting on the steps of his cabin in the work camp, playing his twelve-string guitar, singing the words to Leadbelly's most famous composition, while he waited to catch a glimpse of Andrea LeJeune's purple Ford convertible passing on the dirt road" (164). Robicheaux is haunted not so much by the song as by the image of one convict singing the song of another, waiting for a woman to pass by, a scene at once hopeful and hopeless, and a scene straight out of a blues song.

Later in the novel, Crudup, still in the work camp at Angola, composes a song for Andrea LeJeune, which he calls "The Angel of Work Camp Number Nine." When another inmate berates him for "having t'oughts ain't no nigger in Lou'sana ought to be having" and makes a crude reference to LeJeune, Crudup responds, "She's special 'cause she got respect for other people" (199). Then he plays the first verse of the song:

> At Camp Number Nine it's "Roll, nigger, roll,
> No heaven for you, boy, that state own your soul."
> They took my home and family,
> Give me chains, fatside, and beans,
> Bossman making me a Christian,
> God Almighty, hear that Betty scream.
>
> (200)

Later, he has the opportunity to record eight of his songs, of which this song is the last. When Crudup plays it for Andrea, is has been refined from its original version. He begins to sing it for her:

> White coke and a red moon sent me down,
> Judge say ninety-nine years, son, you Angola bound,
> It's the Red Hat gang from cain't-see to cain't-see,
> The gumballs say there the graveyard, boy,
> If you wants to be free.
>
> Lady with roses in her hair come to Camp Number Nine,
> Say you ain't got to stack no mo' Lou'sana time,
> Gonna carry you up to Memphis in a rubber-tired hack,
> Buy you whiskey, cigars, and an oxblood Stetson hat.
>
> Miss Andrea is an angel drive a li'l purple car,
> Live on cigarettes, radio, and a blues man's guitar—
>
> (205)

At this point, Andrea cuts him off, her face "repelled, as though someone had touched it with a soiled hand" (205). Crudup does not understand when she suggests that he not record the song. Her rejection of him and his song causes him to feel as though "he had swallowed a handful of needles" (206). Clearly, Andrea feels as though he has crossed a line—putting her in the role of both angel and savior, but also making her dependent upon him and suggesting a sense of equality in the way he perceives their relationship, an equality that does not and, seemingly, cannot exist. Crudup returns to her the harmonica she gave him as a gift and asks to go back to the prison camp. In this instance, Burke uses a blues song, a gift from a black convict to a married white woman, to show the inequality that exists between them, and the perceived offensiveness of Crudup's presumption toward LeJeune. That he perceives her as an angel is not the problem per se; that he specifically names her and identifies her as his angel, and as a woman with a role in his future, is the problem in a south Louisiana setting laden with much racial and cultural baggage.

For Crudup, the blues is not just about expressing his own experience. His song conveys the despair and hopelessness of every black man in prison, and of every man of any race who ever wanted a woman he could not have due to racial or class differences. For Burke, the blues represents the entire African American community, with its history of oppression and injustice, much as Cajun music and swamp pop express the communal experience of growing up Cajun.

Music is once again an integral part of *Creole Belle,* one of Burke's more recent Robicheaux novels. Here, though, the emphasis is different. The plot revolves around a collection of songs on an iPod that Robicheaux has been given by a young woman, Tee Jolie Melton, while he is in the hospital recovering from a gunshot wound. Until the end of the novel, the reader does not know whether Melton is alive or dead, especially since certain recordings by Melton herself can only be heard by Robicheaux. As discussed earlier, Burke often connects the song "La Jolie Blonde" with something that used to be, but which is fading and perhaps no longer exists other than in his mind and his memory. Thus it is interesting that Burke chooses to name this woman Jolie, and in fact, one of the songs on the iPod is Melton's recording of "La Jolie Blonde," adding to the multiple layers of meaning. As Robicheaux lies listening to what sounds like French from another time, "I did not realize that I was about to relearn an old lesson, namely, that sometimes it's better to trust the realm of the dead than the world of the quick, and never to doubt the existence of unseen realities that can hover like a hologram beyond the edges of our vision" (238).

However, the song that more deeply informs this novel is Jimmy Clanton's swamp pop hit "Just a Dream," first mentioned by Robicheaux about halfway through the novel as "the light winking on Bayou Teche turned the world into the Louisiana of my youth" (250). The song resurfaces when he visits Clete Purcel at his cottage and asks, "Who's playing that song?" When Clete asks "What song?" Robicheaux explains, "Jimmy Clanton's 'Just a Dream.' You don't hear it?" (327). But Clete doesn't hear it, and wonders if Robicheaux is "coming down with something" (327). However, later, Clete admits: "Dave, I got to tell you something. I don't know if I'm going crazy or not. I heard that song . . . The one you're always talking about. The one by what's-his-name. You know, Jimmy Clanton. 'Just a Dream'? That's the title, isn't it?" Robicheaux responds, "You didn't hear that song, Clete," perhaps not wanting to admit that Clete, too, is ready to acknowledge his own mortality. But Clete insists: "I did. Don't tell me I didn't. I don't believe in that kind of mystical mumbo jumbo, so I don't make it up. It was calling us, Dave" (498). It should also be noted that it is this song that Robicheaux hears coming from a jukebox in the bar next to the café he visits when he is unable to sleep after Annie's death (*Black Cherry Blues* 3). It is as if the song, for Robicheaux, is a reminder of mortality, or the illusion ("dream") that humans have any control over their fate at all.

Throughout the Robicheaux novels, music plays an integral role in both establishing Robicheaux's background and in communicating certain messages and themes. "La Jolie Blonde" becomes not merely an anthem representing Cajun culture, but a song encapsulating Dave's experience as a Cajun from a young boy who used to hear the song on the jukebox or a record player to an old man listening to an iPod, for whom the song has become part of his personal soundtrack. It represents both change and continuity. As the way of life he recalls and longs for has faded, so too has his own life become less distinct. As he hears the blues, he associates it with those who have lived that soundtrack, those for whom life has been a liturgy of sorrow and hopelessness. Jimmy Clanton's "Just a Dream" symbolizes the uncertainty that now seems to devour Robicheaux, as he increasingly begins to doubt his grasp on reality, and on life. Burke uses music in his novels to do more than create a sense of time and place, although it certainly does this; he also uses it to create a sense of longing and belonging. His effective incorporation of music speaks to the sensitivity and strength with which he creates both his characters and their realities.

3
ROBICHEAUX'S ROUX

It is practically impossible to talk about Louisiana without talking about food. The two are often spoken of in the same breath, and no aspect of its culture is so easily and instantly linked to Louisiana as dishes like gumbo and jambalaya, or family and community events like the crawfish boil. These foodways are automatically associated with the state, and often with New Orleans and south Louisiana specifically.[1] While Burke incorporates a variety of cultural elements into his novels, his use of foodways stands out as a central device for highlighting Cajun culture. Burke evokes foodways to demonstrate both how Cajun culture has developed and been sustained in Acadiana and how Cajuns have adapted to their environment. Food at a Louisiana gathering is not merely incidental, it is important. As with music, sometimes foodways can convey information about social and gender roles within the community, and, indeed, sometimes Burke uses food seemingly to reinforce popularly held stereotypes about Cajuns and their world.

It could be argued that when Burke includes examples of local foods, his intention is simply to underline the image of the Cajun as one whose culture is distinguished by distinctive foods and to add, pardon the pun, "local flavor" to the novels. However, looking at Burke's use of foodways in the context of studies done on how food can serve as a self-representative tool for a group of people, it becomes clear that the foods his characters eat are not incidental; rather than merely reinforcing cultural stereotypes, they say something about the culture.

If one were to ask a person from any state other than Louisiana what best typifies or represents Cajun culture, several answers might be anticipated. Among them would certainly be food, closely followed by music. When interviewers talked with those attending the Festival of American Folklife held annually in Washington DC, "food was the most-mentioned marker of ethnic identity" (Kalĉik 33).[2] As a native of Britain, whenever I go back for a visit, I pack my luggage full of British baked goods for the return trip. Not only do I enjoy these foods immensely, but they also help connect me to my childhood and my heritage, bringing to mind times when I lived there and shared these foods with family and friends.

Foods most strongly associated with southwest Louisiana include crawfish and rice, both of which thrive in the wet, marshy terrain (Richardson 14). Like the Native Americans before them, early settlers hunted, fished, and trapped in what would become known as "Sportsman's Paradise," and it has been noted that Cajuns have been particularly innovative in adapting their cuisine to the kinds of meat available in abundance, including "turtle, alligator, nutria, raccoon, possum, and armadillo" (Ancelet, Edwards, and Pitrie 143). More often than not, when Burke depicts a scene including food, it is of a kind locally caught or harvested and then prepared in a way unique to the region. For example, there are many instances in the novels of Robicheaux reminiscing about fishing with his father, and several scenes where he prepares dishes according to family recipes.

Foodways can demonstrate the way racial or ethnic groups have cooperated over time in the evolution of certain dishes. Jambalaya came about as Creoles of European and African descent gathered the ingredients with which they were familiar into a sort of communal pot. Similar to Spanish paella, it combines the local staple, rice, with peppers, spices, and readily available meat or seafood. Jambalaya in Louisiana can be "brown" or "red," depending on the addition of tomatoes. Gumbo, perhaps the food most closely associated with Cajun culture, is also African in origin and is said to be named from the African word for okra, a common ingredient. Jambalaya and gumbo developed as ways to utilize locally abundant food sources and to use up leftovers so that nothing would be wasted in what was often a subsistence economy. Seafood is frequently a key component of gumbo; this practice began in coastal communities where shrimp, crabs, and oysters were harvested in abundance. While not all gumbos contain okra, the base of gumbo is always a roux, a mixture of flour and oil, and the dish often features filé, a powder made from sassafras leaves—this last a contribution from Native Americans to Louisiana cooking (Ancelet, Edwards, and Pitre 142).[3]

It is generally acknowledged that, for the Cajun community, food and its preparation represent more than mere nourishment. Food is not only representative of the culture but a vital part of it. In the short story "Floyd's Girl," by Burke's fellow Louisiana author Tim Gautreaux, when ten-year-old Lizette is kidnapped by the "Texas man," an elderly woman in the south Louisiana community ponders how the little girl will survive without the foods of the region that are such a significant part of her existence. The woman describes foods such as gumbo and turtle sauce piquante as "things that belong on the tongue like Communion on Sunday" (Gautreaux 169) and decides that "living without her food would be like losing God, her unique meal" (169). Food, then, is more than just fuel; it satisfies a cultural and almost spiritual hunger in someone whose life has been sustained by such fare.

In south Louisiana, there is often a performance aspect to the preparation of foods, as evinced by the numerous cooking shows that became popular during the 1990s featuring Cajun fare and bringing to the rest of the country's attention such chefs as Justin Wilson and Paul Prudhomme. The chef, often male, is the chief performer in these folk dramas, with guests functioning as an audience (Ancelet, Edwards, and Pitre 146). Also, food is the defining aspect of many local festivals, from the Rayne Frog Festival to the Breaux Bridge Crawfish Festival to the International Rice Festival at Crowley. These events celebrate the importance of a specific food to a particular community and often mark the historic dependence upon the crop or harvest to the community's survival. Locally available, freshly prepared food is an integral element of many of Lafayette's and New Orleans's festivals as well. A Louisiana festival without food would not truly be a festival at all!

Acknowledging food as a central, tangible element of a culture, Burke uses foodways to demonstrate aspects of the culture in which Robicheaux was raised. In *A Stained White Radiance,* Robicheaux talks to Garrett, a fellow police officer who has just returned from Houston after an investigation by Internal Affairs, a situation that might have soured some toward the area. Robicheaux asks Garrett why he came back to New Iberia, and Garrett responds, "I like it over here. I like the food and the French people" (13). Garrett cites food as one of the reasons he is happy to be back in Cajun country and connects it to the broader culture. Just pages later, Robicheaux sits down to a "smoking bowl of crawfish *étouffée*" (16), prepared for him by his wife. This consists of a local product, crawfish, in a roux-based dish served over rice. It could be argued that the crawfish is the symbol most commonly associated with Cajun culture; it certainly finds its way onto multiple tourist products. Early Cajuns quickly discovered that crawfish abounded wherever there was water—such as in the Atchafalaya Basin and in the rice fields they cultivated. The first crawfish boils were impromptu meals of the "mudbugs" cooked outdoors in washtubs or pots and eaten on the spot (Richardson 14). Leftovers were shelled and used for étouffée ("étouffée" means "smothered").

In a later scene from the same novel, Batist takes some boudin, a spicy rice and pork sausage, out of the microwave. It is then consumed by local fishermen dining at the bait shop. Boudin also makes an appearance in *Heaven's Prisoners,* when Claudette Rocque is flirting with Robicheaux in a not-so-subtle way in front of her husband, Bubba: "She smiled at me, sat at the patio table, crossed her legs, arching one sandal off her foot, and put a piece of *boudin* in her mouth" (92). This could be interpreted as a suggestive gesture since boudin is a type of sausage and the connotation is obvious. However, Burke is also using boudin here to evoke regional foodways. The popular sausage links can be found in most convenience stores and small butcher shops in south Louisiana. It is fair to say that boudin—as well as its cousin, boudin balls—does not have the same appeal for outsiders that such dishes as gumbo or jambalaya have, marking those eating it in the novels as cultural insiders.

In the first of the Robicheaux novels, set predominantly in New Orleans, it is not crawfish étouffée or boudin that is consumed. In *The Neon Rain,* Dave enthuses over a poboy: "I picked up my poorboy sandwich and started to eat. The shrimp, oysters, lettuce, onion, tomato, and *sauce piquante* tasted wonderful" (79). Although now served throughout the southern part of the state, poor-boy sandwiches (often abbreviated to "poboy") originated in New Orleans. Burke ensures that Robicheaux eats foods most representative of the area in order to emphasize the cultural differences between New Orleans and New Iberia. Beignets from New Orleans's Café Du Monde are not part of Robicheaux's home fare when back in New Iberia. Likewise, when he visits Key West, Florida, he notes the smells of the conch fritters, boiled shrimp, and deep-fried red snapper that are specialties of the area (*Heaven's Prisoners* 146). Burke is not alone among authors of Louisiana detective fiction in connecting foods with particular places. In her novel *The Emerald Lizard,* published in 1991 (around the time of Burke's second Robicheaux novel), Chris Wiltz talks about Chef Paul Prudhomme's legendary New Orleans restaurant, K-Paul's, and its popularization of the dish called blackened redfish. She describes how the craze impacted the environment:

> Fishermen were going out into the Gulf of Mexico with closed-at-the-bottom nets called purse seines that they threw over huge schools of "bull" reds, the spawners. Sometimes the catches were so big they couldn't haul all the fish into the boat, so they dumped them back into the Gulf. Unfortunately, fish die in purse seines, so tons of dead redfish were washing up on the barrier islands. The Wildlife and Fisheries got worried about the brood stock. The Feds made purse seines illegal, imposed strict limits on offshore catches and, later, inshore fishing as well. (128)

Wiltz rightly associates blackened redfish with New Orleans, and also mentions the Cajun martini sipped from a Mason jar, "which is how they serve them" (129). So Wiltz, too, identifies certain foods with Louisiana, focusing in on New Orleans, to draw a richer portrait of her setting.[4]

Methods of food preparation can demonstrate gender roles in a community and can also indicate the private or public nature of certain food traditions. The types of food prepared will usually indicate whether the food is to be shared or is for consumption by an individual or the immediate family. In *The Neon Rain,* Burke emphasizes that it is Dave's father who taught him to cook. Robicheaux tells Annie: "My daddy was a wonderful cook. He taught me and my half-brother all his recipes" (61). Not only is it from his father, a roughneck oil-field worker, that Dave learns the art of cooking, a skill usually passed on from mother to daughter rather than from father to son, but it is his father rather than his mother to whom he ascribes ownership of these recipes. This may have much to do with the fact that Robicheaux spent more time with his father than his mother growing up, his mother having abandoned the family at a young age to pursue a dream (and a man) in California.

However, there may be more to this than simple pragmatic reason. As is true in most cultures, women have typically been the domestic cooks in Iberia Parish, and they learn to cook from their grandmothers and mothers, as well as from their mothers-in-law. Men's cooking generally occurs in the public arena, such as at the barbecue or crawfish boil. This tends to support the "performance" aspect of men's cooking, making men the center of attention as they prepare food that, traditionally, they might also have helped to catch. For women, cooking was and continues to be an indoor, private activity shared with other women in the kitchen. So, by making Robicheaux both the cook and the tradition bearer (one to whom recipes are passed and who, in turn, will pass them on), Burke is indirectly pointing to the dysfunction in Robicheaux's family, another element that makes Robicheaux the man he becomes.

Food is often prepared and eaten outdoors in the warm, sunny climate of south Louisiana. In *Cadillac Jukebox,* Robicheaux and Clete Purcel eat lunch at an "outdoor barbecue stand run by a black man in a grove of oak trees" (117), a scene that suggests the necessity for shade in the subtropical temperatures. In the same novel, Robicheaux and current partner Helen Soileau attend a celebratory party in the backyard of Buford and Karen LaRose's New Iberia plantation home after Buford has won a local election. At what could be described as a Cajun version of a scene from Fitzgerald's *The Great Gatsby*, "Hundreds of guests ate okra and sausage gumbo and barbecued chicken wings off of paper plates and lined up at the crystal bowls filled with whiskey-sour punches" as a zydeco band plays from the back of a flatbed truck (200). Barbecue is a food associated with much of the American South, but okra and gumbo give the nod to local foods.

Burke sometimes uses subtle details involving food to draw the distinction between the cultural insider and outsider. For example, in *In the Electric Mist with Confederate Dead,* actor Elrod Sykes invites Dave and his family to join him for dinner at "this place called Mulate's in Breaux Bridge. They make gumbo you could start a new religion with" (45). This is slightly ludicrous in that Sykes, the cultural outsider, advises Robicheaux about a good local place to eat, as though he has more experience and knowledge of the area than Dave. Also, he recommends a local food that Robicheaux could probably better prepare himself from one of his father's recipes. Mulate's is an actual restaurant (as is the town of Breaux Bridge), well known to tourists though often frequented by locals as well. This reinforces Sykes's presumption that he has a greater grasp on the local culture than he actually has.

Gumbo indeed serves as a source and symbol of cultural self-representation in south Louisiana. The question popularly asked when trying to ascertain a person's cultural or family heritage in the area is, "Can you make a roux?"[5] Being able to make a roux, the base of a successful gumbo and a process that requires skill and experience, is seen as a prerequisite for being an "in" member of the culture.[6] So, when Sykes tries to sell the idea of eating gumbo at Mulate's to Dave, he is demonstrating his lack of cultural awareness, his lack of understanding of his role in a culture of which he is not a member. Burke's choice of a restaurant in Breaux Bridge is not incidental. Breaux Bridge is a small Cajun town with a significant minority population of African Americans. Just as gumbo represents the mixture of ingredients from different cultures in the development of Louisiana cuisine, particularly the influence of the Creole culture, so Breaux Bridge represents the mixture of backgrounds, races, and cultures that today make up many southwestern Louisiana towns.

Much more could be said about the varieties of gumbo reflecting different cultural traditions in south Louisiana. Generally speaking, the farther south one goes, the darker the roux. Seasonings also vary considerably. In Cajun prairie towns such as Eunice, basic gumbo might be "spiced only with salt and cayenne pepper [and] served with squirrel, duck, or alligator" (Ancelet, Edwards, and Pitre 35). This reflects the simpler cuisine of rural areas, where hunting is a popular pastime and game is incorporated into many dishes. In fancy New Orleans restaurants, on the other hand, gumbo is more likely to be "flavored with exotic spices [and] loaded with expensive shrimp and oysters" (35); it will also be lighter in color and may even have tomatoes in it, in the Creole tradition. In such restaurants, the consumers are as likely to be tourists as locals. Mulate's in Breaux Bridge would fall somewhere between these two—serving authentic Cajun gumbo in a somewhat touristy atmosphere.

In *Burning Angel,* Burke takes a common southern snack food, cracklings (fried pork skin), and gives it a specifically Cajun French identity. Robicheaux describes the scene when he investigates the damage done by his daughter's pet raccoon to the foodstuffs sold at his bait shop: "I opened the screen door to the shop but hated to look. The jar of pickled hogs' feet was smashed on the floor; half-eaten candy bars, hard-boiled eggs, and cracklings, called *graton* in Cajun French, were scattered on the counter" (44). Enjoyed throughout the South, cracklings even have a special name in Cajun country.

It would be reasonable to say that food is a significant and recognized part of southern culture as a whole, apart from its emphasis in Louisiana, and is therefore an important element in establishing setting in much of southern literature. In an article discussing Kentucky author Bobbie Ann Mason's works, Darlene Reimers Hill states: "Southerners take their food and how they eat it very seriously. Traditional foods and food rituals are important parts of the southern identity" (81).[7] This facet of regional identity has contributed to "family and community solidarity through eating rituals southerners use as touchstones of 'how things ought to be'" (81); these food traditions, "rooted in agrarian necessities, have made for definition, security and stability in southern society" (81). In Mason's stories, as in Burke's novels, food is far more than just fuel; it serves to reinforce group and family identity, together with regional necessity. When Burke uses food to illustrate some facet of Cajun culture, the food's significance marks the culture as southern as well as Cajun.

When Burke mentions food or foodways in his books, he is usually using it to illuminate social status, ethnic background, climate, or some other aspect of the culture. The restaurants where Robicheaux and his family eat are actual local landmarks familiar to those from the area. They tend not to be the generic fast-food restaurants or chains found in Anytown, USA. It could perhaps be argued that Burke's use of Cajun foodways in his novels is somewhat heavy-handed, reinforcing stereotypes associated with the culture. Some may think that foods such as gumbo, étouffée, boudin, and *gratons* have been superimposed into the novels as a way of forcing a cultural context. However, there are more subtle allusions that go beyond the obvious and stereotypical. More than once in *Heaven's Prisoners*, Robicheaux eats something that is not stereotypically Cajun but that is, nonetheless, recognizable within the culture as local fare. As Robicheaux describes a fishing trip, for example, he says, "We'd put cold drinks and sausage, cheese, and onion sandwiches in the ice chest" (272). One mention does not mark a trend, but earlier in the same novel, he buys "a block of cheese, a half-pound of sliced ham, an onion, a loaf of French bread, and a quart of milk in a Negro grocery store" (166). A similar scene occurs in *Burning Angel*. It would be easy to overlook these references because they don't stand out as stereotypical Cajun foods. However, I am assured that ham-and-onion sandwiches (evidently Robicheaux likes to add cheese sometimes, too) are popular among Cajuns and are considered neither odd nor atypical.[8] Occasionally, Burke also includes more generic fare in the novels, such as Grape-Nuts cereal, fried chicken (a southern staple), and snowcones, perhaps to demonstrate that the culture he so carefully portrays is not immune to influence from mainstream America.

Food and music are often served together in Louisiana, as many festivals demonstrate. Both can be considered characteristic of a specific region. Burke's inclusion of foods, and his portrayal of Robicheaux as preparer, provider (as fisherman), tradition bearer, and consumer of regional foods, help once again to situate his protagonist as someone both aware of his cultural background and a living representation of it.

4
BELIEFS ALONG THE BAYOU

Folk belief is an integral element in Burke's novels; Robicheaux is depicted as encountering various forms of folk belief in his dealings with other characters. One of the most notable forms of folk belief in the novels is what may be described as a type of voodoo or conjure, but which is actually more complex than the examples in the novels might suggest. Burke's mingling of folk traditions points to complex belief systems that may be difficult for those outside the culture to access, and the various types of beliefs need some explanation and separation from one another. Burke includes instances of local superstition, of belief in the supernatural and supernatural healing, and of phenomena that cannot be explained rationally. Some of Burke's characters believe in ghosts, some in voodoo, some in faith healing, some in miracles, and some in figures such as the *loup-garou* (the French term for a werewolf). By creating characters who hold and live by these beliefs, Burke not only establishes folk belief as an essential part of the culture but also emphasizes that there is not one common type of folk belief that links all members of the community; neither is it necessarily those lacking in education who hold these beliefs. Robicheaux has experienced other cultures and is something of a pragmatist. However, he is sufficiently in touch with his own culture to know that something does not have to be "true" or scientifically proven for it to be believed in and accepted by those with whom he comes in contact.

Folk belief is usually described as that which is not taught or transmitted through official channels, but which is passed on, often orally, within a group, whether it be a family, a community, or an ethnic group. For example, most schools and churches do not teach that ghosts of dead people come back to haunt the living, but it is a belief that is transmitted through unofficial channels and, perhaps surprisingly, is widely subscribed to.[1] To have some understanding of a culture or a community, it is important to gain insight into the "unofficial beliefs" of that group, although these might be harder to access than the official beliefs. The predominant religion in Acadiana is, and has historically been, Catholicism, but this is by no means the only influence on belief among the Cajuns, Creoles, and others who inhabit the region and Burke's novels. Belief in the *traiteur,* which has its roots in European tradition, and in voodoo, with its roots in African tradition, not only exist side by side but, as portrayed by Burke, can also be different facets of one person's belief system. In fact, the two are often used interchangeably by Burke, in contrast to the typical understanding of these ideas. This is not as unusual as it may appear, given that many people have an "official" belief system to which they subscribe but into which they negotiate other elements that do not directly fit into their primary system of belief and that might even contradict it. Sometimes experience or perception overrides stated belief, and Burke's way of writing these elements helps create an authenticity that sometimes belies conventional understanding.

This mingling, or negotiation, of official and unofficial belief is another aspect of culture that Burke's novels share with Tony Hillerman's stories about Joe Leaphorn. In *Dance Hall of the Dead,* both Zuñi and Navajo beliefs are discussed in some detail, particularly in regard to their differences, but also relevant is the fact that the thirteen-year-old boy who is killed at the start of the novel, and whose death Leaphorn investigates, is described as "an altar boy at Saint Anthony's church, a baptized Christian, a Catholic communicant, a member of a Zuñi kiva fraternity born into the Badger Clan. . . [who] would almost certainly have become one of the 'valuable men' of the Zuni religion" (97). There seems, as in Burke's novels, to be little to prevent a combination of belief systems being not only acceptable but predictable. Both protagonists, Leaphorn and Robicheaux, are pragmatic men, but both represent cultures that allow what may be seen as contradictory beliefs to coexist.

When Burke incorporates folk belief and supernatural occurrences into Robicheaux's experiences, they serve two main functions: they demonstrate the role that these beliefs play in a community and in the lives of individuals in that community; and they establish another element that distinguishes Cajuns and Acadiana from other parts of the United States. If Burke's representation of the traiteur differs from that described by researchers, then it may be that he portrays some of the problems that come with folk beliefs that are, to say the least, fluid rather than fixed. What one person considers a traiteur (translation of the French word for "treater"), another might consider a "quack," and a third a witch or practitioner of voodoo, depending on one's viewpoint. Certainly there are norms to which Burke's characterizations can be compared, but the way in which he uses certain terms requires consideration.

Of the two folk belief systems that Burke portrays frequently in his novels, and that are sometimes present in the same character, the first is voodoo. Voodoo combines elements of African religions with Catholicism, so it is not surprising that this belief system would have thrived in south Louisiana, a region that has a large African American community and where the Catholic religion has been a mainstay since the arrival of French and Spanish settlers. Those who have studied slave religion in the United States have shown that religious ceremonies or rites starting off in one belief system can end up celebrating another with no distinct delineation between the two nor awareness of when that line becomes blurred.[2] What is clear, though, is that when Burke portrays practices consistent with what is commonly perceived as voodoo, he associates them more closely with New Orleans than with Acadiana.

The second folk belief that appears in Robicheaux's world is the belief in the traiteur, and once again, Burke blurs the line between his depiction of the traiteur and the folk tradition as described by those who have studied it. Burke never suggests that Robicheaux adheres to any specific superstition or folk religion, and more often than not his detective shows skepticism toward these practices. Robicheaux does, though, demonstrate that he is open-minded regarding things that cannot be rationally explained. Robicheaux is Catholic, and perhaps his greatest skepticism is directed not toward the practices of the traiteur or even voodoo, but toward those whom he perceives as perverting Christianity—faith healers and televangelists—to take advantage of the naïve and the uneducated. His disdain for such people is demonstrated in his reaction to Lyle Sonnier, a televangelist in the novel *A Stained White Radiance*. Robicheaux describes him thus: "If you flipped through the late-night cable channels on TV and saw him in his metallic-gray silk suit and gold necktie, his wavy hair conked in the shape of a cake, his voice ranting and his arms flailing in the air before an enrapt audience of blacks and blue-collar whites, you might dismiss him as another religious huckster or fundamentalist fanatic whom the rural South produces with unerring predictability generation after generation" (11).

Robicheaux tells his wife: "He takes advantage of poor and uneducated people, Boots. He used the Ethiopian famine to raise money for that television sideshow of his. Look at the car he drives" (19). In a conversation with Robicheaux, Sonnier claims, "I can heal, son," then adds, "I don't brag on it. It's a gift, I didn't earn it" (20), which actually aligns Sonnier's "gift" with that of the traiteur. He explains how it feels to exercise his gift, and concludes: "You can believe it or not, son. But it's God's truth. I tell you another thing. You got a sick woman up in that house" (20). Sonnier's mention of Bootsie's illness, of which he has no previous knowledge, prompts Robicheaux to warn him, "Don't call me 'son' again, and don't pretend you know anything about my family's problems" (20). Sonnier has crossed a line, intruding into his family's affairs, and as much as Robicheaux is tolerant of belief systems that don't line up precisely with his own, his greatest distaste seems to be reserved for those he perceives as contorting the faith to which he does adhere to suit their own needs and to exploit those around them.

Catholicism may be his professed faith, but Robicheaux does not always receive the answers he seeks in the highly organized and institutionalized religion of which he is a part. Often he finds more direction for his own life in the tenets of the Alcoholics Anonymous twelve steps. However, he is quick to correct those who would jump to conclusions when confronted with something they don't fully understand or might misinterpret. In *Dixie City Jam,* one of the darkest of the Robicheaux novels, Batist finds himself a suspect in a series of gruesome New Orleans murders in which the heart of the victim is removed, suggesting a voodoo-esque ritual. When Robicheaux is confronted by Nate Baxter, an old co-worker from his days in the New Orleans homicide unit, he is asked if Batist has ever practiced voodoo. Baxter presents evidence to Robicheaux that suggests his involvement: "You friend wears a dime on a string around his ankle. He carries a shriveled alligator's foot in his pocket. He had bones in his suitcase. The murder has all the characteristics of a ritual killing. If you were in my place, who would be your first suspect?" (35).

There is, however, more than one way to interpret the suspicious items in Batist's luggage. Robicheaux finds an enormous catfish skull in Batist's suitcase (the "bones" to which Baxter refers) and recalls when Batist caught this particular catfish. He explains: "Now when you held up the skull vertically, it looked like a crucified man from the front. When you reversed it, it resembled an ecclesiastical, robed figure giving his benediction to the devout. If you shook it in your hand, you could hear pieces of bone clattering inside. Batist said those were the thirty pieces of silver that Judas had taken to betray Christ. It had nothing to do with voodoo. It had everything to do with Acadian Catholicism" (40). It is interesting that Robicheaux uses the term "Acadian Catholicism"; he is implying that there are elements to the Catholicism practiced and accepted in Acadiana that make it distinct from that practiced elsewhere. Robicheaux also has enough knowledge of Batist's practices and beliefs to recognize the meaning behind the symbolism of the bones. To the uninitiated or the uninterested (in this case, a less-than-agreeable, close-minded homicide cop), they simply suggest voodoo practices, a suspicion reinforced by the fact that the owner of the skull is a black man of limited education. Burke locates this incident in New Orleans, although Batist is a lifelong resident of the New Iberia area, showing how symbols can be open to different interpretations depending on the belief systems prevalent in that locale.

In another New Orleans–based incident, this time in *A Morning for Flamingos,* Robicheaux returns to his apartment to find a large bullfrog nailed to the back of his door, its "puffed white belly split open and its mouth stretched open" (237). Again, the local police appear totally ignorant of what this might mean, seeing only the obvious and not looking beyond the external. They ask Robicheaux jokingly whether he is in a cult.

Dave informs Bootsie, who is with him when he discovers the frog (and the ransacking of his apartment), that the person who nailed the frog to his door was trying to relay a message by putting on, in his words, a "gris-gris show" (240). It is a scare tactic. Robicheaux sees through the show, though, and associates the graphic warning with a person who has "spent some time in a southern jail. A frog with a nail through it means a guy had better jump or he's going to have a bad fate" (240). In this story, Robicheaux has crossed the path of a black woman from Breaux Bridge who goes by the name of Gros Mama Goula. She employs a young black woman named Dorothea who is the girlfriend of escaped convict Tee Beau Latiolais. Burke refers to Goula as a traiteur, but the characteristics with which he endows her are more identifiable as those of a practitioner of voodoo, and the two are usually seen as distinct practices.

The development of these two systems of expression shares some common elements, but the traiteur has traditionally been seen as having its origins in Europe. An individual thought to have the gift of healing uses a combination of prayers and herbs. Often he or she is gifted to heal only one condition, perhaps warts or sunburn, or bleeding. The gift, which is perceived as coming from God, is passed down from one generation to another. Even today, it would not be especially difficult to locate a traiteur, especially in a rural Cajun community, by word of mouth. While not officially recognized by the Catholic Church, traiteurs often consider themselves Catholic and see no contradiction between their practice and the Catholic faith. In this sense, traiteurs can be compared with the curanderas/os of the Hispanic culture, who also walk a fine line between the Catholicism they claim and the indigenous folk beliefs of which they are a part. Typically, though, the powers of the traiteur are seen as being used for positive purpose.

Goula is a powerful woman in her community, but her influence comes not from political or economic power but rather from the ability to manipulate the people who believe she has supernatural abilities. It is claimed that she has put the gris-gris on Jimmie Lee Boggs, a man who shot Robicheaux and almost killed him. The scars this incident caused Robicheaux are both physical and psychological. Robicheaux does not believe in Goula's alleged supernatural power, but he knows human nature well enough to see that her power lies chiefly in what others believe about her. If they believe she has power, then she does, at least over them. When he meets up with Tee Beau, Robicheaux says, "Gros Mama's a juju con woman" (91). Tee Beau is unconvinced by Robicheaux's disbelief and tells Dave: "She put the *gris-gris* on Hipolyte. When he in the coffin, his mouth snap open and a black worm thick as my thumb crawl out on his chin. It ain't no lie, Mr. Dave" (91). Tee Beau's own roots obviously lead him to believe what he has grown up understanding; the traiteur has power, and he believes in Goula's ability to influence people's lives, even reaching them beyond the grave.

Goula's powers appear to have more in common with someone who practices voodoo. In Charles Chesnutt's stories about conjure women, written in the late nineteenth century in the years just after the abolition of slavery, the conjure woman has the power to cripple or kill, to lay a curse and also to remove the curse. The conjure woman of whom Chesnutt writes has much in common with the voodoo priest or priestess, typically a powerful figure in the community, especially among those who subscribe to his or her powers (Burke also refers to Goula as a "conjuror"). These practices also appear in the literature of others who write about the New Orleans area. Robert Olen Butler's more contemporary collection of stories about Vietnamese immigrants living in New Orleans in the years following the Vietnam War includes a story about a man who knew how to deal with his wife's indiscretions while living in Vietnam, but who now learns that the way to exert power in New Orleans is through voodoo.[3] The story is highly amusing, but makes the serious point that voodoo is still seen by some in New Orleans as a powerful medium. In seeking a way to resolve his problems in his new home, the protagonist turns to the supernatural. His "power" in Vietnam was much more pragmatic, as he could have his wife's suitors destroyed by U.S. airstrikes! Since New Orleans has traditionally been a city with a strong Catholic influence, and since many slaves and free people of color resided there in the eighteenth and nineteenth centuries, voodoo naturally flourished in the city, also providing people of color with a means of self-empowerment.

When Burke's characters talk about traiteurs, it is usually with negative connotations. In another passage from *A Morning for Flamingos*, Robicheaux recalls how he has heard stories about Gros Mama Goula from local blacks. The stories describe her as a juju woman who can "blow the fire out of a burn, stop bleeding by pressing her palm against a wound, charm worms out of a child's stomach, and cause a witch to invade the marriage bed" (38). While most of these are positive attributes, and ones that might be associated with the traiteur of today, it needs to be noted that Goula is a character to be feared and someone capable of using her powers for evil should she be crossed. Certainly, studies have shown that traiteurs are acknowledged as having abilities to heal. However, their art is seen as distinct from the practice of voodoo. When describing Goula as a traiteur who also puts spells on people, either Burke is unclear about these distinctions, which is unlikely, or he wants to write a character who represents the "exotic" culture that he creates as part of his setting. It is also possible that he wants to avoid writing Goula as a stereotypical character, striving to make her multidimensional rather than merely depicting her as the typical voodoo practitioner. He may also want to counter the stereotype that the kind of "magic" practiced by African Americans is necessarily malevolent, while that practiced by whites is benevolent. But the fact remains that, even though Goula is undeniably a colorful character, had she been a traiteur in the usual sense of the term, she would have been someone respected within the community rather than feared. That Goula is often referred to as a juju woman or a conjure woman also muddies the waters.

The character of the traiteur reappears in *A Stained White Radiance*. Lyle Sonnier tells Robicheaux that his (Lyle's) father was a traiteur who could cure warts, stop bleeding in cut hogs, blow the fire out of burns, and influence the sex of an unborn child. He also believed in Indian spirits (22). Sonnier's skills overlap with those of Goula, even though the belief in Indian spirits seems to be unique to Sonnier.

The overall effect of Burke's appropriation of the conjure woman and elements of voodoo, no matter what name he gives to the practice, is to provide a sense of place and community in which folk belief not only plays a part but is also widely acknowledged, practiced, and accepted. Even as Robicheaux eschews its actual power, he understands its place in his culture and accepts the influence it can hold over those who believe in it, even as he hides his impatience with what he perceives as ignorance. This can be seen in *Burning Angel,* a novel in which the past and the present are so closely entwined that tangible vestiges of the past keep manifesting themselves. Robicheaux visits Bertha Fontenot, a woman trying to prove her ownership of land that may contain buried treasure. He describes what he sees in front of Bertie's house: "On the planks of the porch I saw a square of red flannel cloth, with a torn root and a tablespoon of dirt in the middle. I saw Bertie watch me out of the corner of her eye as I walked closer to the piece of flannel. Among the grains of dirt were strands of hair, what looked like a shirt button, and a bright needle with blood on it" (181).

Robicheaux understands their significance and says, "I'm going to take a guess—dirt from a grave, root of a poison oak, and a needle for a mess of grief" (181). Bertie neither confirms nor denies his suspicions, and Robicheaux asks, "You think putting a gris-gris on Moleen is going to solve your problems?" (181). Moleen Bertrand is not her ultimate victim, however; later in the novel, Bertie produces an old leather handbag from which she removes "a clutch of pig bones. They looked like long pieces of animal teeth against her coppery palm" (289). She casts the bones onto the table and says: "See, all the sharp points is at the center. . . . Moleen Bertrand dragging a chain I cain't take off. For something he done right here, it's got to do wit' a child, out on a dirt road, in the dark when Moleen was drunk. There's a bunch of other spirits following him around, too, soldiers in uniform that ain't nothing but rags now. Every morning he wake up, they sitting all around his room" (290). Then she predicts, accurately, "Moleen gonna die. Except there's two bones in the middle of the circle. Somebody going with him" (290). However, his companion in death will be Bertie's own daughter, Ruthie-Jean, Bertrand's long-time lover, rather than Moleen's wife, who is the one Bertie really wishes evil upon. Moleen's past, and the past of the land he inhabits, haunt him until his death. Robicheaux puts little confidence in Bertie's use of gris-gris or conjure, but he does appreciate that it has meaning and power for her, and that it is an integral part of her heritage and its accompanying belief systems. And, while she is uneducated, Fontenot is certainly not stupid and has an understanding of human nature that Robicheaux acknowledges and appreciates.

One practice that pervades the novels and that goes some way in explaining Tee Beau's ready acceptance of Mama Goula as a "juju woman" is that of wearing a dime on a string, either around the ankle or the neck, to ward off evil or sickness. In *A Morning for Flamingos*, Robicheaux remembers how Tee Beau's grandmother, Tante Lemon, raised him after he was born prematurely. The baby was "so small it fitted into the shoe box [his mother] hid it in after she put it in the bottom of a trash barrel" (3). Tante Lemon "raised Tee Beau as her own, fed him *cush-cush* with a spoon to make him strong, and tied a dime around his neck with a string to keep illness from traveling down his throat" (3). That Tee Beau survived was probably perceived as proof that the dime had worked its magic. Growing up immersed in such practices no doubt provided Tee Beau with a propensity to believe in the power of the supernatural.

In the first Robicheaux novel, *The Neon Rain*, Robicheaux discovers the body of a young woman while out fishing in Bayou Lafourche. He describes her thus: "She wore a man's shirt tied under her breasts, cut-off blue jeans, and for just a second I saw a dime tied around her ankle, a good-luck charm that some Acadian and black people wore to keep away the *gris-gris,* an evil spell" (10). Here he is describing a young black woman, suggesting that it is not merely the older generations who still hold to this tradition. Batist also "wore a dime on a string tied around his neck to keep away the *gris-gris,* an evil spell" (*Black Cherry Blues* 12). In past generations, it seems that the wearing of a dime was something of a popular tradition, particularly in Creole communities, but it is less prevalent today and probably largely unknown among modern-day Cajuns. Batist has never been outside the state, and his cultural frame of reference is much more limited than Robicheaux's, perhaps having more in common with that of Tee Beau. In a scene from *Heaven's Prisoners,* Robicheaux notes: "Batist was absolutely obsessive about understanding any information that was foreign to his world, but as a rule he would have to hack and hew it into pieces until it would assimilate into that strange Afro-Creole-Acadian frame of reference that was as natural to him as wearing a dime on a string around his ankle to ward off the *gris-gris,* an evil spell cast by a *traiteur,* or conjuror" (58).

Here again, Burke blurs the line between the traiteur and the conjuror, and ascribes to the traiteur the ability and willingness to cause harm, a description that does not mesh with the commonly held perception of traiteurs. Certainly a traiteur who would participate in these actions would be an anomaly since many credit God with their abilities and also refuse payment of any kind—even thanks, since the gift is not theirs. They believe they are only the channel through whom God works. Goula may not be written as a traditional traiteur, but she is written as an interesting, powerful, exotic character and one who adds an element of mystique to Burke's storytelling and to Robicheaux's world.

A person's understanding of his or her own beliefs seldom lines up neatly with descriptions of those beliefs in scholarly works or other "official" explanations. Individually held beliefs veer more toward a combination of the experiential and the inherited. A group of people who claim to subscribe to the same denominational tenets, let alone broad religious tenets, will probably vary in their actual specific beliefs more than might be expected. One reason that folk belief is one of the more complex elements of the Robicheaux novels is that it deals with an aspect of life that is complex. As he incorporates some of the less mainstream expressions of belief in southwest Louisiana into his novels, Burke may not exactly reflect the ways in which those traditions are commonly explained, but what he does do is demonstrate how the lines between belief systems can be blurred as each individual comes to his or her own conclusions—conclusions that sometimes reflect the ideas of the folk group and sometimes tend more toward personal interpretation. Whether Gros Mama Goula is a conjure woman, a witch, or a traiteur, she is undeniably memorable and reflects the multiplicity of conflicting, coexisting belief systems in this part of Louisiana that has been, and remains, home to so many diverse, and sometimes culturally blended, groups.

5
SOMETHING IN THE WATER

Alongside those in Robicheaux's world who actively participate in folk belief systems, be it the traiteur, the practitioner of voodoo, or the wearer of the dime, are those to whom supernatural experiences occur. Robicheaux's belief system, which is by no means limited to conventional Roman Catholicism, allows him to entertain the idea that just as the past is inseparable from the present, so might the line separating the living from the dead be permeable to some degree. This belief is based on Robicheaux's own experiences. Just as the past will not leave him alone, neither will representatives of the past, especially those with whom he has a personal history. While openness to this type of phenomenon may not necessarily be attributed to Robicheaux's cultural background, there is much to suggest that a belief in the supernatural exists among many in the Cajun community. Folk stories persist of the *loup-garou,* the Cajun werewolf, and the *feu follet,* a will-of-the-wisp character. They may be folktales, but they still suggest an openness to the possibility of things that cannot be rationally explained. Also, if belief in the traiteur, a folk healer with some degree of supernatural power, is an accepted part of the culture, then it seems fair to say that other phenomena would not necessarily be ruled out. Also, many cultures allow for a belief in ghosts and spirits that they would not consider part of their day-to-day belief system but that they manage to incorporate when circumstances demand. What makes Robicheaux's experiences especially connectable to southwestern Louisiana is that they typically occur in a water environment, as though the water of the bayou, the thunderstorm, the mist, and the humidity serve as mediums by which these experiences can take place.

Robicheaux's experiences with the supernatural permeate Burke's novels. They are of the type that can be called *memorates,* a term coined by Carl W. von Sydow that can be defined as "first-person narratives about personal experiences" (Honko 103). Lauri Honko takes this idea a step further when she relates memorates to the supernatural.[1] If Burke had merely written Robicheaux as someone who believes in the supernatural but who had no personal experience to back up his beliefs, this would not necessarily be a convincing characteristic and might even prove distracting, making Robicheaux less believable. However, not only does Robicheaux encounter figures from his own past, but the words they speak and the advice and warnings they give have an impact on his views and actions. These experiences influence his behavior—something that Honko says defines a memorate. Also, in Honko's paradigm, the recipient's interpretation of the experience is the only valid one. While Robicheaux does not specifically talk about supernatural encounters, he is aware that what happens to him is unusual and, subsequently, is wary about sharing his experiences with those who might simply ascribe them to his past drinking habits. He chooses his confidants carefully, but there is too much evidence supporting his experiences in the cold light of day for him to explain them away to himself rationally.

In the early 1980s, a folklorist named Gillian Bennett conducted research in a small community in England with regard to matters of a broadly supernatural nature and came to the conclusion that stories regarding personal experience with the dead are more pervasive than have been believed (87).[2] Many of her respondents claimed to have had personal experience of recently deceased relatives, a phenomenon given the term *revenant,* or returner, by folklorist Jan Brunvand (163).[3] Bennett describes two types of revenants: domestic spirits that inhabit a house or other space, and the personal revenant called a "private or familiar spirit" (89); belief in this type of spirit "gains its impetus from the experience of bereavement" (89). The main purpose of such beings is to console in a time of grief or to assist in a time of crisis, and this is the role that Robicheaux's revenants play in his experiences. They also directly link him to his past and his roots, whether the revenant be his father, killed in an oil rig blowout; his deceased second wife, Annie; members of his platoon who were killed in Vietnam; or Confederate soldiers who occupied the same land he currently inhabits. The revenant also serves to "promote the well-being" of its survivors.

Bennett's idea of the revenant existing *alongside* the living is echoed in Burke's own explanation for the supernatural encounters he includes in his novels. In an interview for *The World Over,* a Catholic news program, Burke asserts that his father was a historian who "subscribed to an interesting belief about the nature of history, that it is not sequential or linear, but that all of human history happened simultaneously as in perhaps 'a dream in the mind of God.'"[4] Burke does not say that he holds this view, but it would certainly help to explain how people from different dimensions and time periods can coexist in the same time and place. Also, even if Burke does not subscribe to this idea, he has Robicheaux allude to it when he uses very similar terms in *The Glass Rainbow:* "I sometimes subscribe to the belief that all historical events occur simultaneously, like a dream inside the mind of God. Perhaps it's only man who views time sequentially and tries to impose a solar calendar upon it. What if other people, both dead and unborn, are living out their lives in the same space we occupy, without our knowledge or consent?" (139).

Burke depicts two different types of revenant, but they do not necessarily line up with Bennett's two groups. Burke's may be those with whom Robicheaux was close in life, such as Aldous and Annie, but they may also be Confederate soldiers, as in *In the Electric Mist with Confederate Dead,* or Sonny Boy Marsallus, a small-time New Orleans crook in *Burning Angel.* A preexisting relationship is not necessary but some kind of link is: the soldiers occupied the same piece of land that Robicheaux inhabits one hundred years later. The past haunts and influences Robicheaux in many ways; it can visit him through events, or it can come through the person of a deceased loved one or even a distant acquaintance. All, though, connect him to the past and to the place.

Three of Burke's novels best exemplify Robicheaux's encounters with the dead: *Black Cherry Blues,* in which Annie and Aldous visit him; *In the Electric Mist,* in which Confederate soldiers appear to him; and *Burning Angel,* in which Sonny Boy Marsallus, a criminal believed to have been killed, appears to be protecting the Robicheaux family. However, even in the first novel in the series, *The Neon Rain,* Burke includes a sequence where Dave is sleeping and hears his father's voice. His father tells him, in his familiar Cajun dialect, "*I didn't see him, no.* . . . *That's 'cause I was thinking like me, not like him. That 'gator don't get out on them log when he hungry. He hide under them dead leafs floating next to the levee and wait for them big fat coon come down to drink*" (270).

In response to his father's advice, Robicheaux comments: "I had always thought that I was a good cop, but I was always amazed at how I sometimes overlooked what should have been obvious. My father didn't read or write, but in many ways he learned more from hunting and fishing in the marsh than I had from my years of college education and experience as a policeman" (270). Robicheaux understands that when his father visits him in dreams and offers advice, it is worth heeding. Burke uses very little of this kind of communication between the living and the dead in the first two novels but introduces it early on, emphasizing that this kind of experience is a part of Robicheaux's world and worldview, and laying the groundwork for further incidents, perhaps also gauging his readers' reactions to such incidents. In *Black Cherry Blues,* however, such an experience becomes a significant part of the story as Robicheaux tries to deal with Annie's murder. Annie's communication clearly follows the pattern of that described in Bennett's research as Annie calms, encourages, and advises Robicheaux, providing him with the advice that will help to both keep him safe and solve the crime with which he has been charged. Robicheaux's father also visits him often in his dreams or in a liminal state, between waking and sleeping. Early in the novel, Robicheaux recalls his father's death and how his body was never found, but "even now, almost twenty-two years later, he visited me in my sleep and sometimes I thought he spoke to me during the waking day" (20). He tries to shrug off those visits by saying, "But it's the stuff of dreams. My father was dead. My wife was, too. The false dawn, with its illusions and mist-wrapped softness, can be as inadequate and fleeting as Morpheus' gifts" (20). However, as they become more frequent, and ever more vivid, he is forced to accept these communications as a part of his experience and to heed the warnings and advice offered to him.

The first time that Robicheaux shares a conversation with Annie after her death, it is one in which she delivers a message to him from his father. Previously, advice has come directly from Aldous, but after Annie's death it is she who delivers the message, perhaps because she is the more recently deceased and therefore has less distance to travel between the present and the hereafter. Annie calls Robicheaux "baby love," her pet name for him, and tells him, "Your father's here." Annie and Aldous never met in life since Aldous died many years before she met and married Dave. She continues: "He says to tell you not to get sucked in. What's he mean? You're not in trouble again, are you, baby love? We talked a long time about that before" (38). The conversation is a continuation of, or at least refers to, one that took place between the couple before her death. Robicheaux concludes the conversation by promising Annie that he is coming to see her soon. So disturbed is he by her visits, and by his promise, that he goes to a psychologist, who informs him that they are the result of a death wish. He advises Robicheaux, "I'd get a lot of distance between myself and those kind of thoughts" (38).

The setting for the next encounter with Annie is a rainy night (as later "visits" often will be). He states, "Annie came to me about four a.m., as she often did, when the night was about to give way to the softness of the false dawn" (62). His awareness of the time suggests that this is more than just a dream. This time she tells him she is with members of his platoon from Vietnam. She tells him, "Your buddies from the platoon don't like the rain, either. They say it used to give them jungle sores" (63). Annie relays to him information that he probably did not share with her when she was alive since he would have wanted to protect her from the reality of his war experiences. She asks him if he is drinking, and he tells her "only in my dreams" (63). As he is about to tell her that he wants to join her in death, she interrupts him, saying, "It's not your time. There's Alafair to take care of, too," to which he responds, "It wasn't your time, either" (63). Robicheaux states, "I was sure I felt her fingers touch my lips" (63). For Robicheaux, these conversations are both real and meaningful. It does not seem to surprise him that most of those he has known who have died are together in one place, even though they did not know each other in life. This, after all, is part of his official belief system, which includes belief in heaven (if not a return from heaven). Also, the visits seem not to occur when Robicheaux's life is on an even keel, but when events have created instability and a sense of tension.

Annie's concern about Robicheaux's drinking is an issue in their next conversation. This time, Robicheaux is in jail, suspected of murder, and he tells Annie that, if he weren't in jail, he would be drinking. Then he asks, regarding the murder, "Annie, I didn't do it, did I?" (88). His state of mind is so unsettled that he wonders if, in a rage or a blind drunk, he might have committed the violent crime of which he stands accused. Just as Bennett's informants talk about the reassurances they receive from their revenants, Annie reassures him: "It's not your style, baby love" (88).

In their next encounter, Annie takes him to task for not having attended an AA meeting recently. Again, he alludes to the possibility of joining her, but adds, "I'm Catholic" (118), implying that he does not consider suicide a serious option since it would be a mortal sin according to his conventional belief system. He tells Annie that he is sober and she responds, "But you keep on calling on me. I'm tired, sweetheart. I have to come a long way so we can talk" (118). Here, the implication is that there is distance between the world Annie now occupies and Robicheaux's world. However, it has now been some time since her death, and the distance may be caused by the time passed, suggesting that the longer she is gone, the greater the distance between them. Also implied is that it is he who calls on her, rather than her voluntarily coming to be with him. His need of her is what causes the manifestations to occur, rather than her desire to communicate with him.

Later, in what could be termed a dream scene, Annie and Aldous appear together. Annie advises Robicheaux not to be afraid, to go with his father. Robicheaux responds that he does not want to go with his father, and she reassures him, "We both love you" (217). Robicheaux takes this as a warning that she is about to leave him, but follows her advice and is given further instructions by his father. Later he contemplates the meaning of his dream, stating, "It made no sense to me, other than the facts that I missed my father and Annie, that I feared death, and that I conducted a foolish quarrel with the irrevocable nature of time" (218). However, he still asks the question, "Al, what are you trying to tell me?" (218). Even if he perceives their visits as taking place while he is in a dreamlike state, he takes seriously the advice offered in these conversations.

His next meeting with Annie, perhaps one of the most poignant, is one of his last. This time she advises him, "Listen to the voices in the water" (266). What makes this visit especially poignant is that it happens not when he is sleeping, but when he is fully awake. Robicheaux says: "Then a strange thing happened, because she had never appeared to me during the waking day. But I saw her face in the water, saw the sunlight spinning in her hair" (266).

At the end of the novel, once Robicheaux has exonerated himself, he has one final conversation with Annie. His father is there, too. Robicheaux is out on the marsh at first light and he feels the need to explain his experiences, saying, "I know what I saw that morning, and I know what happened, too, and I feel no need to tell a psychologist about it" (309). Annie tells him: "It's good-bye for real this time, Dave. It's been special" (309). She kisses him on the eyes and the mouth, "as perhaps my mother would have," then disappears into the mist with his father (310). After that experience, "Neither sleep not late-night thunderstorms bring them back" (310). Robicheaux's crisis is, at least temporarily, over. He solves the crime of which he has been accused, and his life takes on some semblance of normalcy once again, but still Robicheaux acknowledges that there are times when he thinks of "voices that can speak through the rain and tease us into yesterday" (310).

Robicheaux's encounters with Annie postmortem prove that he is open to supernatural experiences that defy rational explanation, and also that these are somehow a part of a worldview that he can accept. Bennett's subjects ascribed several attributes to the deceased who remained a part of their lives; among these were an "awareness of the concerns of the living, powers of communication, and a sense of purpose" (92). Each of these is present when Annie visits Robicheaux. She knows he is in trouble and is aware of his past troubles; she is able to communicate clearly with him using words and, occasionally, touch; and she offers him advice and comfort for his current circumstances. She continues to maintain contact with Robicheaux until the conflict has passed and he is able, however unwillingly, to function without her.

The next series of supernatural events appears in the aptly titled novel *In the Electric Mist with Confederate Dead*. Here, Robicheaux's belief in this type of experience is reawakened by an encounter with actor Elrod Sykes, who is in New Iberia to make a movie set during the Civil War. When Robicheaux pulls Sykes over for driving under the influence of cocaine, Sykes tells him that he has seen the remains of a body and asks, "Does anybody around here ever talk about Confederate soldiers out on that lake?" (7). Robicheaux suggests they are actors, maybe to convince himself as much as Sykes, but Sykes is insistent and tells him that they are "shot up real bad" (7). Sykes concludes the conversation by telling him: "You believe when most people don't, Mr. Robicheaux. You surely do. And when I say you believe, you know exactly what I'm talking about" (8). Sykes recognizes in Robicheaux a kindred spirit, someone that he senses not only understands the things he sees, but also sees them himself.

Later, Robicheaux tells Sykes that in the years when he was drinking, he believed that dead people (from his Vietnam platoon) would call him up on the telephone. On some level, Robicheaux still wants to disassociate himself from these metaphysical experiences, and especially from Sykes's knowledge of them. But Sykes continues to describe the Confederate soldiers he has seen, complete with lanterns hanging from their ambulances and maggots in the wounds of the soldiers to eat out the infection. Robicheaux tries to ignore Sykes's words, and eventually Sykes concedes that he might have been drunk because of a particular detail that makes no sense to him. The general with whom he has conversed tells Sykes that Robicheaux's father has the revolver that belonged to his adjutant, Major Moss. Sykes asks, "How could your father have his adjutant's pistol?" (52). At mention of his family, Robicheaux stops the conversation, but later he goes to a shoebox filled with things from his childhood, including what he refers to as "the best gift my father ever gave me" (53). The pistol has the name J. Moss engraved on the trigger guard, a fact that Sykes could not have known.

Sykes is not the only one who sees the soldiers. Alafair and a friend, Poteet, are playing in a later scene when Alafair asks Robicheaux, "Dave, who was that old man?" (172). The girls describe him as a man with a stump for a leg and an arm like a shriveled-up bird's claw, walking with a crutch. They also mention his strong body odor, and his coat that is "gray with some gold on the shoulders" (128). If his father had possession of the adjutant's gun, then it would appear that the soldiers at one time occupied the land where Robicheaux's family have made their home. It is as if the whole family shares a connection with the soldiers, and with the past they represent, the land being the point of connection.

Robicheaux first encounters the soldiers himself when he has been attending a party given by the film crew. He suspects that his drink might have been spiked, but this is speculation, and while driving home in a thunderstorm he runs his truck off the road. In spite of his confusion, he feels compelled to walk in a certain direction and soon sees for himself what Alafair and Sykes have been describing to him. Robicheaux attests: "The men around the fire paid me little notice, as though, perhaps, I had been expected. They were cooking tripe in an iron pot, and they had hung their haversacks and wooden canteens in the trees and stacked their rifle-muskets in pyramids of fives. Their gray and butternut brown uniforms were sunbleached and stiff with dried salt, and their unshaved faces had the lean and hungry look of a rifle company that had been in the field a long time" (159). Then Robicheaux spots the man Alafair had described to him: "His left arm was pinned up in a black sling, and his right trouser leg flopped loosely around a shaved wooden peg. He moved toward me on a single crutch. I could smell tobacco smoke and sweat in his clothes. Then he smiled stiffly, the skin of his face seeming almost to crack with the effort. His teeth were as yellow as corn. *'I'm General John Bell Hood. Originally from Kentucky. How you do, suh?'* he said, and extended his hand" (160).

A conversation ensues between Robicheaux and the general during which, for a moment, Robicheaux believes he might be dead. He tries to convince Hood that the war is over, but Hood tells him, "*It's never over. I would think you'd know that. You were a lieutenant in the United States Army, weren't you?*" (162). When Robicheaux tries to tell Hood that he gave that war "*back to the people who started it,*" Hood insightfully tells him, "*No, you didn't. It goes on and on*" (162).

Hood then tells Robicheaux not to give up his cause. When Robicheaux says that he does not understand, Hood tells him, "Our bones are in this place. Do you think we'll surrender it to criminals, to those who would use our teeth and marrow for landfill?" (163). As Robicheaux is about to leave, he asks the general, "It's going to be bad, isn't it [. . .] something that's waiting for me down the road" (163). But Hood claims to have "more insight into the past than the future" and can offer little more than platitudes.

The next day, Robicheaux is found in his truck cab and taken to the local hospital. The doctor detects no alcohol in his system but suspects LSD. However, on returning to the scene of the encounter, Robicheaux finds the remains of a campfire. He digs around a little and discovers a scorched brass button, the bottom of a hand-blown bottle, and, finally, the remains of a surgeon's saw. He decides not to share his finds with anyone, rationalizing that "the general and I would not share our secrets with those whose lives and vision were defined by daylight and a rational point of view" (173). Robicheaux knows that what he has seen and found cannot be explained rationally, even though Sykes and his own daughter have experienced the same phenomenon. What is interesting is that, in this situation, he aligns himself with the irrational and is aware of this fact.

As Robicheaux becomes increasingly aware that his own family is in jeopardy, the general tells him, "Keep the Sykes boy with you" (239). In his encounters with the general and the other soldiers, all the signs point to a physical presence having been there with him, rather than merely a spiritual presence. In a later incident, when Robicheaux is left in a state of semiconsciousness, two soldiers physically help him to his feet—they are flesh and blood. Also, the general warns Robicheaux that his family might be at risk, a function in line with Bennett's description of the revenant.

Later, in a state of half-sleep, Robicheaux sees the general descend in the basket of an observation balloon of the type used during the Civil War. Robicheaux is mourning the loss of a friend from the police department, Lou Girard. Girard's death has been ruled a suicide, but Robicheaux suspects otherwise. The general advises Robicheaux, "Listen to me very carefully, lieutenant. No matter what occurs in your life, no matter how bad the circumstances seem to be, you must never consider a dishonorable act as a viable alternative" (271). The general and Robicheaux part on disagreeable terms, as if neither can completely understand the other, or the world they are forced to cohabit.

Toward the end of the novel, Robicheaux has his penultimate visit with the general, who laments lives lost in the war, and Robicheaux tells him, "People don't get to choose their time in history, general" (318), an interesting perspective since it seems that Robicheaux, with his longing for the past, could just as easily be talking to himself. The general, Robicheaux, and the soldiers stand for a photograph before the general departs.

Their final meeting occurs when Robicheaux is attempting to rescue Alafair from her kidnappers. Robicheaux sees the general briefly in the full beams of his truck headlights. He warns Robicheaux, "Don't use those whom you love to justify a dishonorable cause" and reminds him that he gave the same advice to Sykes (333). Robicheaux is undeterred, even though this is not the first time this advice has come his way. As he is attempting to capture Doucet, Alafair's abductor, the general makes one final intrusion into Robicheaux's life. As Doucet is fleeing, "A wooden crutch that looked hand-hewn, with a single shaft fitted into the armrest, sprang from under his boot and hung between his legs like a stick in bicycle spokes" (337). Doucet falls and is killed by Robicheaux's temporary partner, Rosie Gomez. After ensuring Alafair's safety, Robicheaux offers the crutch up into the air, saying, "Don't you want to take this with you, sir?" (339). There is no response. It is as if the general has done what he came to do in Robicheaux's life and can now leave him alone. He has done what the revenant is known to do: warn of impending danger and protect from harm. In what is almost a postscript to the story, Robicheaux, Alafair, and Bootsie are looking at a book from the public library about the "War Between the States." Alafair asks Robicheaux, "What are you doing in here, Dave?" She shows him a picture in the book and says, "You're in the picture. With that old man Poteet and I saw in the corn patch. The one with B.O." (345). Robicheaux sees the picture of the general, the men, and himself, although he does not acknowledge that it is, indeed, he who is in the picture along with John Bell Hood and his men.

In the Electric Mist with Confederate Dead effectively demonstrates Burke's belief that the past and the present can never really be separated from each other, that there is no particular time or place where one ends and the other begins. In Burke's writing, the past and the present are intertwined, and one is affected by the other. This is especially true in instances where there are issues from the past that have never been resolved and where past wrongs have not been accounted for or redressed. The Confederate general's presence in Robicheaux's life seems to derive from the fact that his men inhabited, however briefly, the same land that Robicheaux's family has inhabited for several generations. So both the land itself as a physical entity and the space it represents serve as a connecting point for Robicheaux. It also appears that, the two men both being soldiers, they share a common experience that binds them together and enables them to have empathy for each other, even if they do not see the world the same way.

It may well be that Robicheaux's attachment to the past, and his tendency to romanticize the past, make him a likely recipient for visits from revenants and ghosts. In wanting to hang on to what has been, and effectively being transported to a different time whenever he hears a particular song or visits a specific, meaningful place, he opens himself up to those from the past who desire to make contact with him. Also, experiences he had, or thought he had, while under the influence of alcohol have made him aware that sometimes things occur that cannot be rationally explained. He is less inclined to deem something impossible, knowing that he had unusual experiences while not fully in touch with reality, such as when dead members of his platoon in Vietnam would call him on the telephone while he was drunk.

The soldiers, and especially General Hood, fulfill many of the prescribed functions of the revenant. However, in *Burning Angel*, a novel where the present and the past are again inextricably intertwined, the question posed both to Robicheaux and the reader is, is Sonny Boy Marsallus alive or dead? If dead, then how is he still involved in Robicheaux's life and looking out for his family? Marsallus is a small-time crook with mob connections but, when he is shot and runs toward the ocean, presumably to die (for in many of Burke's novels, water both gives and takes life), his body is not found. Robicheaux ruminates, "I couldn't accept Sonny's death. People like Sonny didn't die" (203), but his assertions are based more on guilt over Sonny's death than on fact. He does not want Sonny to be dead lest he played some role in his demise. His thoughts about Sonny torment him as he tries to rationalize what happened: "They didn't find a body, I told myself. The sea always gives back its dead, and they didn't find Sonny's body" (203). Marsallus's background does cause a person to consider whether, in fact, Sonny belongs to that group of people that seem indestructible, immortal even. Early in the same novel, Robicheaux's former partner, Clete Purcel, describes how he and Marsallus served together as mercenaries in South America. He tells Robicheaux: "Sonny was on point.... I saw this.... I wasn't hallucinating.... Two guys next to me saw it, too" (37). Purcel continues: "He got nailed with an M-60. I saw dust jumping all over his clothes. I didn't imagine it. When he went down, his shirt was soaked in blood. Three weeks later he shows up at a bar in Guatemala City. The rebels started calling him the red angel. They said he couldn't die" (36). From the outset of the novel, Marsallus's questionable status regarding whether or not he is alive is established. He is described as having very pale skin, suggesting a ghostlike appearance. Purcel also informs Robicheaux: "There's something not natural about him. . . . He doesn't get any older. He always looks the same" (65), implying that Marsallus has been frozen in time, in youth, perhaps remaining at the age he was at his death.

After Marsallus's reported death in the shooting incident, an old "friend," the disease malaria, which he contracted during his time in Vietnam and which still lives in his body, revisits Robicheaux. In a state that could be described as delusional, he is visited by Marsallus, who invites him to feel the exit wounds left by the bullets that hit him. It is a scene reminiscent of the New Testament story in which the resurrected Christ invites his disciples, especially the doubting one, to feel the wounds left by the nails used in his crucifixion. Perhaps both have returned from the dead. This is not the only time that Sonny seems to take on attributes of Christ. These include a fondness for the Virgin Mary, whom he has tattooed on his body, and his efforts to help prostitutes leave a life of prostitution, even at the risk of incurring wrath from those who profit from their lifestyle. His name, too, suggests a link to "the Son." Robicheaux tries to dismiss the visit, during which Marsallus attempts to assuage Dave's guilt over his death. Upon waking, though, he finds a piece of seaweed at his feet, presumably deposited there by Marsallus. Just as the Confederate soldiers leave evidence of physical presence in *In the Electric Mist with Confederate Dead*, so Marsallus leaves tangible evidence of his actual presence, rather than a purely spiritual presence.

When it appears to Robicheaux that Marsallus has taken on a protective role concerning Robicheaux's family (much as the general did), he tells Bootsie: "It's not my job to explain the unexplainable. St. Paul said there might be angels living among us, so we should be careful how we treat one another. Maybe he knew something" (324). His Catholic faith wants to explain what happens in terms of a belief system that he can understand. At the culmination of the action, when Robicheaux is helpless and Bootsie shoots their assailant, it is because of a mysterious telephone call that Bootsie knows what is taking place and what she needs to do. Robicheaux tries to reassure Bootsie that she did what she had to do, and that if she hadn't picked up Clete's phone call, he would be dead. But Bootsie tells him that it was not Clete who called. "The phone rang out in the garden and he said, 'Dave's in trouble. I can't help him. It's too far to come now. You have to do it'" (333). This occurs after Robicheaux has seen Marsallus's body in the morgue and identified him by his tattoo of the Virgin Mary. Bootsie, though, knows what she heard, and tells Dave: "You said you saw his tattoo on the remains in the morgue. You swore you did. But I know that voice, Dave. My God" (334). She knows who it was that saved Dave from death. Marsallus tells her on the phone that he cannot help; it is "too far" for him to come. Just as Annie grew exhausted coming back to help her husband, so Marsallus has to reconcile himself to being more a part of the dead than the living. Still, he is able to help Robicheaux one final time.

Dave's rescuers always seem to come when he is totally unable to help himself. Sonny rescues him when he has a gun pointed at the side of his head, and again when he is debilitated by malaria. Annie assists him when he cannot solve the crime of which he is accused. The general aids him when his daughter is in the hands of kidnappers. Perhaps it is when Robicheaux meets the end of his own abilities that he is open to help from wherever it can come. A similar phenomenon occurs in *Jolie Blon's Bounce*. A soldier by the name of Sal Angelo, the name suggesting some kind of angelic being, attaches himself to Robicheaux in the role of protector, whether or not Robicheaux wants his help. He claims to know Robicheaux from his time in Vietnam, but Robicheaux doubts this. It is significant that Angelo's name implies angelic protection since another character in the novel is called Legion, a name given in the New Testament to a man possessed by so many demons that their number becomes his name.[5] Ultimately, Legion avoids the gunshots that should have ended his life, but is instead struck down and killed by lightning. When the action reaches a climax, Legion confronts Sal Angelo "as though recognizing an old enemy" (345), an obvious reference to the recognition of good by an evil being. Legion ends up "floating around with a bunch of dead pigs" (346), another reference to the biblical story of Legion in which the demons leave the afflicted man's body at Christ's command and enter a herd of pigs, a type of livestock considered "unclean." The pigs then rush off a cliff and are drowned. At the close of the novel Robicheaux states: "I never again saw the ex-soldier who called himself Sal Angelo. I didn't want to think any more about his coming to New Iberia, virtually out of nowhere, dressed in rags and madness, or his claim that it was he who had carried me on his back out of the elephant grass and loaded me onto a helicopter bound for battalion aid. What did it matter who he was?" (348). As is characteristic of Robicheaux, though, he finds himself unable to let the matter go and requests information from the Veterans Administration. From them he learns that "a soldier named Sal Angelo, from Staten Island, New York, had indeed been a medic in my outfit and had served in the same area as I in late 1964 and early 1965. But one month after I was hit, he had been killed ten miles from the Loation border" (348). Once again, a figure from Robicheaux's past, and one with whom he has no personal relationship, has chosen to come back through time and from death in order to help Robicheaux when his life is threatened. And the case can be made that Burke's revenants are strongly linked to the roles ascribed them in Bennett's research, in which "the dead are thought to return during a crisis to afford protection and advice, to promote health and peace" (92).

In Burke's novels, the element of water usually serves as a connecting point between the revenant and Robicheaux. For Burke, water is not only an integral part of the environment in which Robicheaux grew up, but a force of life. Louisiana, and especially southwestern Louisiana, does not suffer from a shortage of this commodity. The very air itself is saturated with water, the humidity levels being so high, and water is a dominant feature in both the landscape and the lifestyle, even the foodways, of Acadiana. The Atchafalaya Basin is made up of acres of swampland and waterways; the Gulf of Mexico meets the land along its southernmost edge. It is not surprising, then, that Burke would utilize this element in his stories. He endows water with a certain liminal quality. It is used both as a means of offering life and as a conduit for the dead to visit with the living, as if water is the means of transportation and transition between life and death. Catholics and other Christian denominations use water in baptism to signify death to the old life and a new life in Christ. So, in the religion dominant in Acadiana, water symbolizes a connection between life and death; it is a purifying source, also, in that it symbolically washes away the past and the old or sinful nature. In *The Glass Rainbow,* this idea is applied to the state itself when Robicheaux ruminates during a thunderstorm: "To me, the rain in Louisiana has always worked as a kind of baptism. It seems to have the same kind of restorative properties, washing the dust from trees and sidewalks, rinsing the pollutants out of our streams, giving new life to the grass and flowers, thickening the stalks of sugarcane in the fields. When it rains at night in Louisiana, I remember the world in which I grew up, one that came to us each morning with a resilience and clarity that was like a divine hand offering a person a freshly picked orange" (109).

Burke uses water at especially significant moments in his works, whether it be in Robicheaux's remembrances of his father dying in the Gulf in an oil rig accident; Sonny Boy Marsallus rising, as if reborn, from the ocean; or his daughter being "given" to him from an air pocket amidst the murky waters surrounding a sunken, crashed airplane. Annie dies during a fierce rainstorm and returns to him in watery visions. Water provides a final resting place for Aldous and also tries to claim the life of his adopted daughter, just as it has claimed the little girl's mother. Instead, though, it "offers her up" in an almost sacrificial manner, as if she is rising to a new life from the cloudy depths that more commonly take from Robicheaux rather than give to him.

The waters of south Louisiana claimed not only Robicheaux's father, but also the body of his mother. Mystery surrounds her death until the story comes to light in *Purple Cane Road*. Robicheaux remembers working, as a young man, on an offshore seismograph. The year is 1957, "the year Hurricane Audrey pushed a tidal wave out on the Gulf of Mexico on top of Cameron, Louisiana, crushing the town flat, killing hundreds of people" (99). He recalls that bodies were found in the water for weeks after that, but one day as he was working, he disturbed a pocket of cold air trapped inside the root system of a tree and "suddenly the body of a woman rose out of the silt against mine, her hair sliding across my face, her dress floating above her underwear, the tips of her fingers glancing off her mouth" (100). In his dreams, the woman becomes his mother, and two cops are pursuing her as she runs past fields of purple sugarcane. A surge of water from the Gulf roars toward her, and she trips and falls. Roots wrap around her body, and the water engulfs her until the current closes over her.

In dreams, Robicheaux connects incidents from the past, like Hurricane Audrey, with the unknown: the death of his mother, the details of which he has never learned. He fears that she worked as a prostitute and knows something of her indiscretions, but it is not until he talks to a woman by the name of Caledonia who used to be a prostitute at the place where Mae Guillory, his mother, waited tables, that he learns the truth about his mother's occupation at the time of her demise. Caledonia assures him that his mother was "no working girl," and describes what she recalls about his mother's death. Mae witnesses two police officers trying to blackmail her boss, Ladrine Theriot, and when she laughs at them, they return two nights later in the midst of a violent rainstorm, often a predictor of violence in Burke's writing. Mae is unable to hear what is said, but her boss's face is "bloodless" as they leave. Their visit and their words visibly shake him. He then turns in the gangsters who are ruining his life. Mae is impressed by her boss and thinks they may run off together, but Caledonia tells her, "He growed up here. Coon-asses don't go nowhere. You gonna die, woman" (243). When Theriot does not come for her, she goes after him and witnesses his death at the hands of two policemen. They see her and later come for her. When she refuses to deny what she has seen, they kill her and roll her body into the bayou, so that water claims the body of his mother just as it has his father.

Robicheaux believes that, just as his father's bones and hard hat and boots are still out in the Gulf, so is his "brave spirit" (321). He also believes that his mother's body, which was never found, drifted from the bayou into the Gulf and that "she and Big Al were together under the long, green roll of the Gulf, all their inadequacies washed away, their souls just beginning the journey they could not take together on earth" (322). Robicheaux understands their inability, as flawed people, to make their marriage work, but he sees the waters of the Gulf as healing, cleansing, the means by which imperfections can be washed away. The water provides a second chance for their relationship, just as Alafair is given a second chance when she is offered up by the Gulf, and Dave is given a second chance at having a family with his new wife and adopted daughter.

In one of the later novels, Robicheaux returns to the idea of his parents reuniting in death, and a vision of them occurs that has been a long time in the making. Again, Alafair is in danger and Dave and Clete are risking their lives to rescue her (together with Clete's daughter, Gretchen). As he approaches a hut, the sound of dry leaves beneath his feet reminds Dave of going squirrel hunting with his father. He ponders: "I wondered where Big Aldous was. I wondered if he was with my mother and if they were both watching over me, the way I believe spirits sometimes do when they're not ready to let go of the earth. My parents had died violent deaths while they were young, and they knew what it meant to have one's life stolen, and for those reasons I had always thought they were with me in one fashion or another, trying to do the right thing from the Great Beyond" (*Creole Belle* 511).

Here, Robicheaux's thoughts on the matter are more concrete than in previous instances, as if in his older years he is more willing to accept what cannot be explained and to give credibility to the unknown. As he approaches the cabin where he believes he will find his nemesis, he experiences the following:

> Then a strange occurrence took place, maybe one that was the result of a cerebral accident inside my head. Or maybe I experienced one of the occasions when we glimpse through the dimension and see the people to whom we thought we had said good-bye forever. Inside an envelope of cool fire, right on the bank of the bayou, like the flame of a giant votive candle, I saw my mother, Alafair Mae Guillory, and my father, Big Aldous Robicheaux, looking at me. She wore the pale blue suit and the pillbox hat with the stiff veil she had always been so proud of, and Big Aldous was

wearing his tin hat and hobnailed work boots and freshly laundered and starched PayDay overalls, his arms covered with hair as thick as a simian's. At first I thought my parents were smiling at me, but they weren't. Both were waving in a cautionary way, their mouths opening and closing without making any sound, their faces stretched out of shape in alarm. (511)

It is then that Clete calls out a warning to Dave, and Dave suffers a flesh wound in the ensuing gunfight. It is the first time he has seen his parents together in this way. Usually his father comes to him alone, and the lack of visits from his deceased mother might be connected to the lack of knowledge about her death or the sense of abandonment he felt in his relationship with her. On this occasion, though, his parents are united and return from death together to try to protect their son from a premature death like theirs.

Usually, though, it is in the Gulf waters that Robicheaux "meets" his father in the years after his death. The following is a typical scene: "I saw him walking out of the surf, the green waves and foam sliding around the knees of his overalls, his powerful body strung with rust-colored seaweed. . . . I could feel the saltwater surge over my legs as I walked towards him" (*Black Cherry Blues* 20). It is both a physical and spiritual experience, and his father's death is closely linked with the place where it happened.

In perhaps the most vivid recollection of an encounter with his father, just before he is visited by Sonny Boy Marsallus, Robicheaux thinks about his father and ruminates on his watery death:

> I knew the spot by heart; I could even feel his presence, see him in my mind's eye, deep below the waves, his tin hat cocked at an angle, grinning, his denim work clothes undulating in the tidal current, one thumb hooked in the air, telling me never to be afraid. Twice a year, on All Saints' Day and the anniversary of his death, I came here and cut the engines, let the boat drift back across the wreckage of the rig and quarterboat, which was now shaggy with green moss, and listened to the water's slap against the hull, the cry of seagulls, as though somehow his voice was still trapped here, waiting to be heard, like a soft whisper blowing in the foam off the waves. (*Burning Angel* 270)

Robicheaux throws yellow roses into the water at the spot where his father was killed, in a scene and a gesture somewhat similar to that used by the helicopter pilot Robicheaux mentions later in the novel who floats statues of Jesus to those killed when the helicopter went down. Both demonstrate a belief in the ability to reach the dead via the water and, somehow, offer consolation.

When Annie visits Robicheaux after her death, it is almost always at a time of intense rainfall or storm conditions. In one encounter with her, it is raining hard at night and Annie comes to him in the soft light of the "false dawn": "I could look though my bedroom window into the rain, past the shining trunks of pecan trees, deep into the marsh and the clouds of steam that eventually bleed into the saw grass and the Gulf of Mexico and see her and her companions inside a wobbling green bubble of air" (*A Morning for Flamingoes* 63). It is also within a bubble of air that he finds Alafair, in the cockpit of the submerged plane. Robicheaux makes the connection. In one of his darkest moments, he despairs that Annie's visits have become less frequent, "and her voice had grown weaker across the water and in the din of the rain" (258). But, he consoles himself, "I had Alafair, who was given to me inside a green bubble of air from below the Gulf's surface" (258). Also, when he eventually sees Annie in the light of day, he sees her face in the waters of a stream.

In the Electric Mist with Confederate Dead provides an example of the power that water holds to bring the past into the present. The title itself, of course, refers to a damp atmosphere suffused with moisture that can conceal as well as reveal. Robicheaux recalls a time when he was working in the Gulf for an oil company and witnessed what he believed was the murder of a black man. As he tries to escape, the man stumbles into the water, and Robicheaux never sees him come up, although he tries to convince himself that the man might have been able to hold his breath long enough to elude his killers. He states, "At age nineteen I did not want to accept the possibility that a man's murder could be treated with the social significance of a hangnail that had been snipped off someone's finger" (11).

The water holds the body for a long time, keeping it submerged as it lies and decomposes in the root system of a tree, and Sykes discovers it as the water level recedes. As Robicheaux tries to find out what happened back in 1957, he tells the prison guard who had been holding the murdered man: "Sometimes rivers give up their dead, Mr. Hebert. In this instance it took quite a while" (183).

In the case of Sonny Boy Marsallus from *Burning Angel*, it is the ocean that seems to consume Marsallus, then returns him to those who need his protection. As his assassins approach, he runs for the beach and into the waters of the ocean, and as the gunshots hit his body, he struggles into the water to die. When Robicheaux is considering the probability of Sonny's having died in this incident, he states, "I dream that night of people who live in caves under the sea. Their arms and shoulders are sheathed in silver feathers; their abalone skins dance with fiery sparks" (213). Then he recounts the story of a helicopter pilot he knew from Morgan City who had been flying wounded civilians to safety in Vietnam when they crashed in the middle of a river; most were burned or drowned. Robicheaux tells the pilot's story thus:

> He became psychotic after the war and used to weigh and sink plastic statues of Jesus all over the waterways of southern Louisiana. He maintained that the earth was wrapped with water, that a bayou in the Atchafalaya Basin was an artery that led to a flooded rice plain in the Mekong Delta, that somehow the presence of a plastic statue could console those whose drowned voices still spoke to him from the silt-encrusted wreckage of his helicopter. When he hung himself, the wire service story made much of his psychiatric history. But in my own life I had come to believe in water people and voices that can speak through the rain. I wondered if Sonny would speak to me. (213)

The recent novel *Light of the World* includes the same ideas. This novel, set in Montana, includes a lengthy passage that begins, "I have always loved and welcomed the rain, even though sometimes the spirits of the dead visit me inside it" (255). Dave reminisces about his childhood and Louisiana's summer weather patterns and the predictability of the showers that would come through almost every afternoon. He describes how children see rain as a friend and understand its "baptismal nature, the fashion in which it absolves and cleanses and restores the earth" (255). He continues: "The rain also brought me visitors who convinced me the dead never let go of this world. After my father, Big Aldous, died out on the salt, I would see him inside the rain, standing up to his knees in the surf, his hard hat tilted sideways on his head. When he saw the alarm in my face, he would give me a thumbs-up to indicate that death wasn't a big challenge" (256). But it is Annie that features most strongly in this recollection as it becomes even more focused: "The person who contacted me most often in the rain was my murdered wife, Annie, who usually called during an electric storm to assure me she was all right, always apologizing for the heavy static on the line" (256). Then he shares his views on these experiences: "Don't ever let anyone tell you this is all there is. They're lying. The dead are out there. Anyone who swears otherwise has never stayed up late in a summer storm and listened to their voices" (256). His certainty that the dead remain and inhabit, or are transported by, the rain, remains consistent from the first novel to the most recent.

Throughout his works, Burke suggests that water is more than simply a plentiful element in southwestern Louisiana. Just as it is essential to life, so in Burke's stories it has the ability to link the living and the dead, perhaps because of its fluid nature. Although Bennett's research on revenants lacks this element, when Burke introduces a revenant into Robicheaux's life, it is done with water as the vehicle for that person's journey, whether it be through a rainstorm, a lightning storm, a river or stream, an ocean, or the saturated night air.

Inherent in Burke's use of folk belief and the supernatural is the idea that folk belief is an innate part of the life of a community and the individuals that make up that community. Whether he is writing about Batist wearing a dime on a piece of string, or Gros Mama Goula's reputation as a person with supernatural power, or Bertha Fontenot's predicting the future by casting bones, or whether he is relating Robicheaux's experiences in the mist with a Confederate general, or a more intimate conversation with Annie in a rainstorm, Burke suggests that, in this Acadian community, supernatural occurrences and beliefs are a natural part of the worldview. This, in turn, suggests a place with strong links to the past and a place where modern pragmatism is not the only option. It is a place where different racial and ethnic groups provide a combination of beliefs, much as they provide the basis for the food and music that distinguishes the area. Robicheaux might balk at the hold that Goula has over certain members of her community, but he does not doubt the validity of the advice given by his dead father. Both Goula and Robicheaux understand that not everything can be rationally explained, no matter a person's level of education or experience. What is clear is that when Burke's readers read about such beliefs and experiences, they are being offered another glimpse of the culture and environment that surrounds Robicheaux. It is another aspect of Burke's writing that piques the interest of his readers, encouraging a deeper interest in the culture and the locale, and providing further information on Dave Robicheaux's world.

6
FIGHTING THE GOOD FIGHT
FOLK JUSTICE AND SOUTHERN VIOLENCE

Readers familiar with him will acknowledge that Dave Robicheaux is a violent man. His father was a violent man who enjoyed a good brawl when he got back from a stint on the oil rigs, perhaps as much a way to relieve tension as anything else. It was a part of everyday life, and is an aspect of oil-field culture explored by other writers, such as Tim Gautreaux, several of whose short stories address the violence endemic to oil towns like Morgan City. Robicheaux's drinking has also led him into situations that he can neither explain nor remember, and his experiences in Vietnam have both reinforced and redefined his attitude toward violent acts. Also, his partner and friend Clete Purcel does little to discourage what to him comes as naturally as breathing, the result of growing up the son of a violent man in a violent environment. But, as Robicheaux explains in *Creole Belle,* in their maturity there are some rules that guide Dave and Clete's use of violence: "Clete protected the innocent and tried to do good deeds for people who had no voice, and I tried to care for my family and not brood upon the evil that men do. We didn't change the world, but neither were we changed by it" (528).

The type of violence endemic to Burke's Robicheaux novels is what scholars have labeled southern violence, a type that pertains as much to region and history as to acts themselves. Of course, as an example of the hard-boiled detective, Robicheaux is expected to react violently in certain situations. John Cawelti, who puts forth a set of criteria that the hard-boiled detective will exhibit, states that he "sets out to investigate a crime but invariably finds that he must go beyond the solution to some kind of choice or action" (142), which frequently involves the hero in "violence, deceit, and corruption that lies beneath the surface of the respectable world" (145).[1] Burke's books, while falling into the detective fiction genre, also fall into the genre of southern fiction. Not only do they feature a specific southern setting, but the influence of the past is felt strongly and informs the novels. As demonstrated in the previous chapter, this influence of the past can at times manifest itself as a physical presence, sometimes as a spiritual one, and often in social terms.

Several scholars distinguish southern violence as a particular type of violence. It is rarely gratuitous, but comes from a place of cultural significance and expectation. John Shelton Reed asserts that, in terms of random acts of violence, the South is no more dangerous than anywhere else. Where crime excels in the South is in terms of personal grudges, where perpetrator and victim know each other. Most are familiar with the post–Civil War feud between the Hatfield and McCoy families, and it is this kind of personal interaction that not only results in violence, but also leads to a perpetuation of violence when a like response is considered the norm. As Reed states, "Arguments and lover's quarrels and family disputes are dangerous business in the South"; he contends that "the homicides in which the South seems to specialize are those in which someone is being killed by someone he (or often she) knows, for reasons that both the killer and the victim understand" (144).[2] There is little that is random about these acts, and no one aware of the situation is especially surprised when they occur.

In keeping with the characteristics of southern violence, when Robicheaux becomes violent, it is usually a reaction to a deeply personal matter, or to a situation in which the person he confronts has hurt or threatened someone incapable of self-defense. Robicheaux's use of violence is never random; even if he does not mean to react as violently as he does, there is a cause for his reaction. Robicheaux sees violence as the last resort of a civilized person and never seems proud of the times when he is forced to use it. He is, though, capable of extreme violence when the situation warrants it. When debating how he will deal with his wife's killers in *Heaven's Prisoners*, he states: "Guns kill. That's their function. I had never deliberately kicked a situation into the full-tilt boogie. The other side had always taken care of that readily enough. I was sure they would again" (162). In other words, he does not need to initiate a violent response because those responsible for his wife's death would undoubtedly force a situation where the only appropriate and effective response would be one of a similar ilk. Robicheaux will not need to "deal the play," but neither will he back down when a score needs to be settled. A southern man cannot do so if he wants to be considered a man.

Heaven's Prisoners has many violent incidents, including the murder of Robicheaux's wife and a brawl of the kind that he probably knew his father to be involved in. This one is between Dave and someone he grew up with, Bubba Rocque. A fight for Robicheaux is usually a fair fight; he is unlikely to shoot an unarmed opponent and follows certain rules about what is acceptable and what is not, rules that he learned growing up among oil-field workers and other blue-collar men in south Louisiana in the 1950s. When someone he cares about is hurt, he will exact justice, not revenge. When he discovers that bartender Jerry Falgout has betrayed his friend Robin, and that Robin's finger has been broken and her life threatened, he pays a visit to Falgout, runs Falgout's face into a window fan, and then pulls his .45 on him (76). The punishment fits the crime according to his sights: He injures the man and lets him know that there could be worse, reflecting that done to Robin. His response is both personal, because Robin is his friend, and retaliatory, because Robin is a woman and cannot defend herself against men who are physically stronger. This falls within the acceptable boundaries of southern violence, which is in many ways akin to the Old Testament "eye for an eye" justice meant to put limits on acts of retaliation.

Later in the same novel, Robicheaux kills the two men who murdered Annie. My choice of words here is deliberate, killing being the result of a violent conflict between two parties who come together to settle a dispute, murder being an act of unprovoked violence. Robicheaux's actions represent the kind of killing permitted by the southern culture, in which a set of shared values allows such a response to such an act. The death of his wife is personal to Robicheaux, and he resorts to a personal response that members of his community would probably not only tolerate but condone. Robicheaux's actions would not be considered extreme, given the situation, nor would he be considered a bad person for pursuing this course of action. Folklorist and oral historian William Lynwood Montell explores this idea and finds that those he interviewed who had knowledge of local killings in the upper South region "viewed the killers as law-abiding, moral beings, not unlike other area residents, and people looked upon violence in a matter-of-fact way" (144).[3] These are not random acts of violence carried out by someone unknown within the community, but violent acts committed by those with reason. In fact, they would be seen as reasonable acts. Robicheaux's killings did not occur during the commission of a robbery; also, they are acts of justice, not of revenge. They rectify the situation rather than facilitating or furthering it. As far as the community is concerned, the murderers deserve their fate because their act of violence, surprising a sleeping woman alone in her home and shooting her, is unacceptable and violates cultural norms; Robicheaux's retribution and killing fulfills cultural norms. It is also worth noting that Louisiana is a state in which the death penalty not only exists but is used.

Robicheaux, in this instance, joins the Iberia Parish Sheriff's Department before pursuing the murderers. He could have acted as a vigilante and brought the men to a kind of vigilante justice, but instead pursues them while representing the law and wearing a badge. In their study *Cajun Country*, Ancelet, Edwards, and Pitre trace the history of folk law and justice-related violence back to the days preceding the Louisiana Purchase, stating that the isolation the Acadians experienced in the swamps led to a great degree of independence and resulted in finding their own way of settling disputes. This type of folk justice is not dissimilar to that practiced by the descendants of the Scotch-Irish who settled the Appalachian region. Once the Louisiana Territory became part of the United States, the Acadians often found themselves at odds with established legal authority. Civil authorities frequently chose not to confront the Acadians to enforce their regulations. Besides, many of the disputes were territorial, exacerbated by strong community ties, and the system of justice that the Acadians had formed often precluded the involvement of outside authority, an idea that tended to prevail into the twentieth and, arguably, the twenty-first centuries. Their findings confirm Reed's, as Ancelet states that in south Louisiana, "people involved in violent situations usually know each other and usually understand why they're at odds" (110). Ancelet et al. cite the dance hall as the focal point for community and territory-related violence in the early twentieth century. Feuds between families added fuel to an already potentially volatile situation as young men and women from different families, and sometimes different communities, literally and figuratively "stepped on each other's toes" at the dances. Faced with either closing down or finding a way to maintain order, dance hall owners resorted to deputizing the toughest fighter by pinning a badge on him, and putting him in charge of maintaining order. These men, who were already predisposed to violence, could now fight as long as it was on the side of the law (107).

In much the same way, the Iberia Parish sheriff hires Robicheaux, perhaps against his better judgment, because he knows that Robicheaux can bring Annie's killers to justice and maintain order. He knows that Robicheaux wants to wear a badge in order to bring justice to his wife's killers. He also knows that these men will probably not see the inside of a jail cell. Still, the sheriff recognizes his own inability to deal with the killers, and even recognizes the necessity of going beyond the law, although he warns Robicheaux against taking matters into his own hands: "I can't believe you haven't come to some conclusions. I wouldn't want to feel you're being less than honest here, and that maybe you're going to try to operate on your own after all" (142). If this were really his fear, however, knowing Robicheaux and his personal involvement with the case, the sheriff would not entrust him with a badge. But the sheriff tells Robicheaux candidly: "I'll be truthful with you, Dave. I don't know where to start on this one. We just don't have this kind of crime around here" (143). The sheriff knows that this kind of crime does not conform to culturally accepted norms, so he pins a badge on the toughest guy around, who happens to be Robicheaux. He can now fight on the side of the law while doing what official law enforcement cannot.

Robicheaux's use of violence rarely exceeds that which is necessary for the situation. In fact, he often stops short of what might be acceptable according to cultural norms. In *The Neon Rain,* the pattern is established as he pursues Philip Murphy, a thug who killed an FBI agent and also tortured and attempted to kill Robicheaux. He corners Murphy in a duplex, and when Murphy tries to surprise him with a concealed weapon, he shoots and kills Murphy. Later he says, "I would never be able to decide whether the second shot was necessary" (230). As he watches Murphy die, he admits, "I took no joy in it" (230). Robicheaux has no interest in and no appetite for revenge, just justice. In an incident from *A Morning for Flamingos,* Robicheaux is shot and left for dead by Jimmie Lee Boggs, an escaping convict. The rest of the novel involves Robicheaux's attempts to track down Boggs and confront the man who not only threatened his life but also humiliated him. When the opportunity to exact revenge presents itself, Boggs is trapped beneath a vehicle under rising water. Robicheaux could kill him or leave him to die; instead, he tries to save him. Boggs dies anyway, but not by Robicheaux's hand. Neither does Dave kill Claudette Rocque, the woman whom he discovers was behind Annie's murder. In this instance, he lets the justice system take over, although this may have more to do with his code of ethics toward women, another aspect of his upbringing. It is interesting to note that in *Burning Angel,* when his life is threatened by a woman holding a gun to his head, it is his current wife, Bootsie, who pulls the trigger. Perhaps it is more palatable for a woman to kill another woman than for Robicheaux to enact this kind of violence, however justified.

In general, Robicheaux tends not to have much faith in the justice system, even as, or perhaps especially as, a representative of that system. He expresses his ideas to the Confederate general who haunts him in *In the Electric Mist with Confederate Dead.* Robicheaux asks General Hood what would happen to men who rape and beat women in his day, and the general assures him that they would be arrested, tried, and hanged (although, of course, it could be argued that aspects of slavery suggest otherwise). Robicheaux tells him, "You wouldn't find that the case today" (272). He reiterates this point in *Heaven's Prisoners:* "The fact is that most criminals are not punished for their crimes.... If you want to meet a group of people who have a profound distrust of, and hostility toward, our legal system, don't waste your time on political radicals; interview a random selection of crime victims, and you'll probably find that they make the former group look like utopian idealists by comparison" (144).

He knows there are too many times when dangerous criminals go free due to bureaucratic glitches and a justice system that can fail victims of violent crime. In a scene from *Black Cherry Blues,* he makes the point personal when he tries to get the police to help him when Alafair's well-being is threatened. In typical Robicheaux style, his past experience influences his attitude toward the ability of law enforcement to deal with the matter effectively. He describes the scene from the perspective of the victim: "Maybe you've been there ... your body is still hot with shame, your voice full of thumbtacks and strange to your own ears, your eyes full of guilt and self-loathing while uniformed people walk casually by you with Styrofoam cups of coffee in their hands. Then somebody types your words on a report and you realize that this is all you will get" (61). Taking matters into one's own hands, especially if the authorities seem unwilling or unable to mete out justice themselves, is a course of action that, in Montell's words, derives from "deep rooted historical and cultural factors" in the South (162). He explains:

> Area residents seemingly learned from historical experience, and from cultural inculcation through imitation and molding during childhood and early adult years, to accept killing as a means of settling disputes; they seemingly permitted such acts as long as the culturally bound parameters were adhered to; they learned to live with the ever-present possibility that a member of their own family might be involved in homicide as a killer or victim, depending on the situation, and they learned the art of forgiving the aggressor. (162)

This idea is borne out in the works of many southern writers, including Lee Smith (who explores Appalachian culture, both in the present and the past) and Tim Gautreaux, albeit at times without the element of forgiveness mentioned by Montell. One of Gautreaux's short stories, "Floyd's Girl," concludes with the "Texas man" who has kidnapped Floyd's girl being ejected from a cropduster after having an eye put out by a granny with her walker and having his truck dismantled! A scene from Smith's *Oral History* has Dory Cantrell, daughter of moonshiner Almarine Cantrell, recounting almost without emotion the moment her father was killed by business rival Paris Blankenship, and asserting that the apron stained with his blood won't be washed until her brothers have avenged her father's death. It is not a suggestion, that it *might* happen, but a certainty that it *will* happen. Indeed, it does. Certainly, descriptions of Robicheaux's experiences growing up at least allude to the code described by Montell. Robicheaux and his brother were often left alone while their father went drinking and brawling in bars. They learned that there were times when fighting was not inappropriate. We are given this insight into Robicheaux's background in the first novel in the series, *The Neon Rain*, perhaps to establish an aspect of Robicheaux's worldview. An incident is described in which Dave and his brother Jimmie are working at a bowling alley resetting the pins, a job often reserved for African Americans. Robicheaux recalls: "A group of tough kids who lived down by Railroad Avenue came in and started rolling the second ball before the pin boy could reset the rack. These were kids who went nigger-knocking on Saturday nights with slingshots and marbles and ball bearings. The Negroes in the pits couldn't do much when they were abused by drunks or bad high-school kids, but Jimmie imposed no restraints upon himself and always practiced immediate retaliation" (64).

Robicheaux then describes how one of the kids sent a bowling ball sailing past Jimmie's kneecap, and then does it a second time. Jimmie proceeds to put a wad of used chewing tobacco into the thumbhole of a bowling ball and to seal it with bubble gum. He continues: "A moment later we heard a loud curse, and we looked out from under the racks and saw a big, burr-headed boy staring at his hand with a horrified expression on his face. 'Hey podna, smear some of it on your nose, too. It'd be an improvement,' Jimmie yelled" (65).

This incident results in a violent brawl between Jimmie, Dave, and some of the boys from the bowling alley who clearly look down on the Robicheaux boys for taking what they consider a demeaning job. Robicheaux states: "Three of them caught us in the parking lot after the alley closed and knocked us down on the gravel for five minutes before the owner came out, chased them off, and told us we were both fired. Jimmie ran after their truck, throwing rocks at the cab" (65). There was no calling in the cops, no indication that this was unexpected behavior, and the incident ended there. All involved, in Montell's words, "tolerated violence within well-established limits as a method of maintaining social order" (162).

Robicheaux's self-imposed limits on violence might be a result of his experiences in Vietnam, or his self-awareness regarding his drinking. They might even stem from his Catholicism. Whatever the case, the violence depicted in Burke's novels usually occurs when two parties who know each other come together to confront the other, each knowing that violence can result. When violence intrudes from the outside, when it is conducted in a way not condoned by cultural norms, then all bets are off and Robicheaux has to be prepared to fight as dirty as the competition, especially when others' lives are at risk. This is especially strongly demonstrated in scenes where Robicheaux's family is threatened. The violence is written in such a way that it accords with studies on southern violence and also illustrates the way of life that Burke attempts to create—one in which "folk justice" has its place. Even Batist, a man rarely associated with violence in the novels, demonstrates his understanding of the need for personal action when Alafair's life is threatened in *Black Cherry Blues*. Although he cannot read the letter that contains the threat, he understands the accompanying photographs and asks, "What we gonna do?" (57). Not used to perceiving Batist as a champion of vigilante justice, Robicheaux explains that he will pick up Alafair from school, then talk to the sheriff. But Batist persists, "No, I mean what we gonna *do*?" and Robicheaux notes: "His brown eyes looked intently into mine. There was no question about his meaning" (57). Batist is making clear his willingness to go the extra mile in order to protect a child, especially a child who has already witnessed so much violence in her life, and a child for whom he has an almost paternal affection.

Burke makes the case for southern violence in such a way that, when Robicheaux is paired with someone from outside the culture, it can result in a conflict of opinions. Clete Purcel, Robicheaux's partner from his days in New Orleans with whom he unofficially works even after Purcel is expelled from the force, never questions either Robicheaux's methods or his motives. Purcel is a product of New Orleans's rough-and-ready Irish Channel and is no stranger to the concept of taking personal responsibility for exacting revenge when sinned against. When Dave's life is threatened in *Black Cherry Blues,* it is Clete who comes to the rescue. Robicheaux's attacker, a hired hit man named Charlie, described by "the total absence of moral light in his eyes" (213), is taken by Clete, but not to the police station. When Robicheaux tries to ascertain the man's fate, Clete tells him: "You don't need to know any more, Streak. Except the fact that our man didn't like heights" (231). In fact, Robicheaux is often seen as the restraining influence when Purcel's violence threatens to erupt and exceed even Robicheaux's boundaries, although Clete does suggest that he is willing to do what Robicheaux *wants* to do but will not allow himself to do. But when Robicheaux is paired with a female detective from the FBI and someone from outside his area, the lines become questionable and blurry. Toward the end of *In the Electric Mist with Confederate Dead,* Alafair is kidnapped by Murphy Doucet, and Robicheaux believes that a mob-connected producer of pornographic films, the oddly named Julie Balboni, knows Doucet's whereabouts. Robicheaux discusses his course of action with his temporary partner, Rosie Gomez, who asks him, "What are you going to do if you catch Doucet?" (325). Robicheaux responds, "That's up to him," but Gomez already knows him well enough to suspect that he has only partially answered the question. She states, "I saw you put something in your raincoat pocket when you were coming out of the bedroom" (325), suggesting that he has concealed a weapon with which to deal with Doucet.

Gomez is an outsider, not from the South, and she works for the

FBI. She is a former migrant worker from Mexico via the migrant camps of Bakersfield, California, who has clawed her way up to a respectable job in law enforcement. She does things by the book, and it seems as if she does not fully understand the "southern" way of dealing with matters, especially where family is concerned. Their inability to reach common ground on the correct way to proceed demonstrates Gomez's lack of understanding of what, to Robicheaux, is the accepted way of doing things. She asks for his word that his mission to rescue Alafair is not a "vigilante mission," and Robicheaux's response demonstrates the differences in their expectations for dealing with the situation: "You're worried about *procedure*. . . . In dealing with a man like this? What's the matter with you?" (326). The complete lack of understanding on Gomez's part is made clear by the question, and the complete lack of appreciation of why vigilante justice would be inappropriate is expressed by Robicheaux. He cannot fathom why procedure could possibly matter when his daughter's life is at risk. Not only does he not trust procedure, he does not trust those who would choose to abide by it when more direct action, albeit outside of the bounds of the law, will probably succeed in getting the job done of rescuing Alafair. It is the same behavior he exhibits when dealing with Annie's killers. His response is personal, because his daughter's life is at risk; and it is retaliatory, as she is a child and cannot defend herself.

On the journey to Doucet's camp in the Louisiana bayous, Robicheaux and Gomez again state their positions. Gomez says, "I'm not sure you're in control anymore." For Robicheaux, though, the point is that he is in control because he can control the action in a way that others cannot. He explains: "The army taught me what a free-fire zone is, Rosie. It's a place where the winners make up the rules after the battle's over. Anyone who believes otherwise has never been there" (332). She acquiesces, and agrees to say no more.

When Robicheaux confronts Balboni, he is angered by Balboni's lack of concern for his daughter ("Hey, maybe you can get her face on one of those milk cartons") and reacts to the perceived lack of respect: "I handed Rosie the shotgun, put my hands on my hips, and studied the tips of my shoes. Then I slipped an aluminum bat out of the canvas bag, choked up on the tape handle, and ripped it down across his neck and shoulders. His forehead bounced off the mirror, pocking and spiderwebbing the glass like it had been struck with a ball bearing. He turned back toward me, his eyes and mouth wide with disbelief, and I hit him again, hard, this time across the middle of the face" (329). When this fails to produce the required effect, Robicheaux takes the gun from Gomez and continues on his violent course toward Balboni until he has the information he needs regarding Doucet's whereabouts. Ultimately, and ironically, it is Gomez who shoots and kills Doucet, absolving Robicheaux of the responsibility. But Robicheaux rescues his daughter, knowing that he would have crossed any line placed there by the law, or procedure, to do so. Gomez demonstrates the difference between those who believe that "doing things by the book" is always right and those, like Robicheaux, who are convinced that sometimes that is neither sufficient nor effective.

Ultimately, Burke includes violent incidents in his novels because his characters inhabit a violent world—the world of the hard-boiled detective in a southern setting. He combines elements of both southern literature and the detective fiction genre to create stories that strike a chord with readers who want to identify with a world in which wrongs are righted and the good guy does indeed win in the end. Robicheaux satisfies the reader's need for both a southern gentleman and a knight in shining armor, and does it while providing an appropriate southern response to situations that call for one. Burke's readers and Robicheaux's followers have come to expect nothing less.

7
NEW IBERIA

DAVE ROBICHEAUX'S HOMETOWN

Like most of us, Dave Robicheaux is a product of his environment. That his hometown of New Iberia is so frequently referenced in the novels, and in such vivid detail, suggests that this is a place close to his heart. It is a place with more than mere memories attached to it but with experiences ingrained, experiences that have helped make him the man that he is. New Iberia, though, is more than just a setting. With it, James Lee Burke has taken a small, virtually unknown southwestern Louisiana town and both revealed it to the world and created an identity for it in which to situate Robicheaux. It is a town that has its flaws, much as Robicheaux does himself, and it is a town that represents almost as much what it is *not* as what it is.

It is not, for example, New Orleans—a much bigger city with a distinctly different culture and different issues associated with it. Writers such as Chris Wiltz and Julie Smith write about the unique entity that is New Orleans. New Orleans is also part of Robicheaux's formation and a place that he has chosen to reside in for a time, but it lacks the maternal aspect that New Iberia provides for him. Neither is New Iberia the Atchafalaya Basin, a place that Dave associates with miscreants and others who choose to live life "below the radar," many of whom flout the law along with any form of outside authority. While aspects of its independence might appeal to Robicheaux, those who inhabit the Basin in Burke's novels relish their abandonment of any kind of order to a degree that even exceeds Robicheaux's tolerance. New Iberia is not even Lafayette, the closest city of any size to New Iberia and the town in which ULL (the University of Louisiana at Lafayette) or, at one time, SLI, Robicheaux's alma mater, is located. Robicheaux has mixed memories associated with Lafayette; as home to the Oil Center, it symbolizes the industry that has been a source of environmental and other problems affecting especially the poor and uneducated in the state, even as it has brought economic growth and jobs. New Iberia is also not Baton Rouge, the state capital and home of the politicians (and many of the televangelists) whom Robicheaux instinctively mistrusts.

No, New Iberia is none of these places. It's a town divided, sure, between rich and poor, those that had money and land before "the war" (specifically here the "War between the States") and those who never had those things and probably never will. It is a town with historic, and contemporary, racial divisions. It is also a town that has undergone significant change from the time when Dave was growing up. It now has a Wal-Mart and McDonald's and drive-through daiquiri stands, but it still serves as a refuge for Robicheaux from New Orleans, the Atchafalaya Basin, Baton Rouge, and even Lafayette. It is, and always will be, home, and through the novels, readers too have come to appreciate New Iberia and to see it almost as an additional character in the stories, a character as full of southern charm and latent hostility as any other.

What sets Burke apart from other writers of detective fiction who have also chosen a distinct location for their novels is the way in which Robicheaux describes his hometown and the obvious affection he has for New Iberia, in spite of its shortcomings. Robert B. Parker's Spenser may admire Boston, even love it, but apart from mention of a visit to Fenway Park sparking reminiscences of visits with his father, his affection is largely unspoken. Certainly he knows the city, but his connection appears more on a surface level than at the root-deep level of Robicheaux's unequivocal affection for New Iberia, which he describes in great sensory detail.

Cajun culture gained popularity during the 1980s largely because America has become increasingly homogenous since the 1950s and the Cajun culture offered something foreign, exotic, and different that Americans could experience without having to leave American soil. Hollywood movies, together with cooking shows by the likes of Justin Wilson and Paul Prudhomme, played their part in making the culture accessible, even if the movies put their own less-than-positive spin on how the culture would be portrayed. *The Big Easy* brought to the screen a group of people who had their own music, food, and language, as well as their own, often dishonest, way of doing things. The movie is set largely in New Orleans but features a detective, Remy McSwain, who is identified as Cajun at least on his mother's side. Foodways, music, occasional Cajun phrases, and other cultural markers accentuate the distinction, even as it could be argued that the movie blends Cajun and New Orleans culture in a rather inaccurate way. *No Mercy* showed a culture that made its own rules and that seemed to bear little relation to the reality of the lives of most Americans at that time. The fact that the Cajun character in *No Mercy*, a crime kingpin who "owns" the glamorous but uneducated and almost childlike character played by Kim Basinger, led a life totally unrelated to that led by the vast majority of Cajuns in Louisiana or elsewhere was, seemingly, irrelevant to the movie makers or moviegoers. The movies sold an image that made Cajun culture seem dangerous as well as desirable, where rules were meant to be broken, if indeed they existed at all, and people could live life on their own terms. *No Mercy* and *Southern Comfort* showed more of the culture Burke associates with residents of the Atchafalaya Basin than of friendly towns like Lafayette and New Iberia. *Southern Comfort* in particular depicts Cajuns as being unsympathetic to outsiders. In this movie, a group of National Guard reservists on exercise in the Louisiana swamp run afoul of local Cajuns by stealing their pirogues. When confronted, the Guardsmen fire blank ammunition to scare off their pursuers but find their fire returned with live ammunition. As the situation escalates, the Guardsmen are ill equipped to deal with the unfamiliar terrain in which the Cajuns are so completely at home. In an era of Reaganomics and yuppy get-rich-quick-schemes, the rawness and earthiness exhibited in movies such as these was, for some, irresistible. The fact that this culture could be found within the continental United States made it even more attractive because it was at once both foreign and attainable.

James Lee Burke would be the first to admit that when he created Dave Robicheaux in the 1980s, he had no idea how popular the series would become. On the advice of a friend, he decided to try his hand at detective fiction, although he says that, fundamentally, *The Neon Rain* differed little from his previous works; the main change was in the occupation of the protagonist. So, when he began writing about Robicheaux and decided, at the conclusion of the first novel, to have him move back to New Iberia, he could not have anticipated that people would want to know more about this small town in southwestern Louisiana that Dave Robicheaux calls home.

If Burke's books have made a hero out of their main character, they have also made something of a celebrity of the town in which many of Robicheaux's adventures are set. Robicheaux spends time in New Orleans, Lafayette, Florida, and Montana (where Burke also has a home), but it is New Iberia that dedicated readers associate with Robicheaux, and the place they are most likely to want to visit when attempting to track down the "Robicheaux experience." This is hardly surprising when readers are regaled with descriptions of the town's beauty and southern charm, such as this taken from *A Stained White Radiance:*

> East Main in New Iberia is probably one of the most beautiful streets in the Old South or perhaps in the whole country. It runs parallel with Bayou Teche and begins at the old brick post office and the Shadows, an 1831 plantation home that you often see on calendars and in motion pictures set in the antebellum South, and runs through a long corridor of spreading live oaks, whose trunks and root systems are so enormous that the city has long given up trying to contain them with cement and brick. The yards are filled with hibiscus and flaming azaleas, hydrangeas, bamboo, blooming myrtle trees, and trellises covered with roses and bugle vine and purple clumps of wisteria. In the twilight, smoke from crab boils and fish fries drifts across the lawns and through the trees, and across the bayou you can hear a band or kids playing baseball in the city park. (47)

Certainly, in such a lavishly descriptive passage, it seems that this is not merely any southern town but one for which the orator, Robicheaux, feels a deep affection. He describes it with great sensory detail, making it seem almost Edenic given its lush foliage. The trees themselves are uncontainable and will take on the newer, man-made elements of the town, and win. And even if, at times, Robicheaux is willing to divulge less-palatable parts of New Iberia's history, he acknowledges that his feelings for this town are somewhat conflicted. He states in the same novel, "No matter how educated a southerner is, or how liberal or intellectual he might consider himself to be, I don't believe you will meet many of my generation who do not still revere, although perhaps in a secret way, all the old southern myths that we've supposedly put aside as members of the New South" (265). He continues, stating that as a child he had access to few books, but still grew up knowing about "General Banks's invasion of southwestern Louisiana, the burning of the parish courthouse, the stabling of horses in the Episcopalian church on Main Street, the union gunboats that came up the Teche" (265). He concludes: "Who cares if their cause was just or not? . . . you realized that they died right here in this field, that they bled into this same dirt where the cane would grow eight feet tall by autumn and turn as scarlet as dried blood" (265–66). Robicheaux's South, his New Iberia, has seen its share of turmoil but still represents, for him, a place of safety and comfort, a place he can retreat to when New Orleans (where the series of novels begins) becomes too much. Even the land between the two is distinct from his home. To get from New Orleans to New Iberia he must cross the Atchafalaya Basin, another place that he describes in detail:

> The Atchafalaya basin is the place you go if you don't fit anywhere else. It encompasses hundreds of square miles of bayous, canals, sandspits, willow islands, huge inland bays, and flooded woods where the mosquitoes will hover around your head like a helmet and you slap your arms until they're slick with a black-red paste. Twenty minutes from Baton Rouge or an hour and a half from New Orleans, you can punch a hole in the dimension and drop back down into the redneck, coonass, peckerwood South that you thought had been eaten up by the developers of Sunbelt suburbs.

It's a shrinking place, but there's a group that holds on to it with a desperate and fearful tenacity. (144–45)

Although in its wildness and lack of civilization this is a place that also tends toward a pristine state of nature, the basin seems always to contain nature run amok and uncontrollable, much like the people who choose to reside there. It is violent like New Orleans, but in a more organic, less organized way. It seems to represent some kind of perilous landscape that Robicheaux must cross in order to reach his Valhalla.

Robicheaux also describes the Atchafalaya in terms of the independence and/or rejection of rules and authority that can be attained there: "There are not many places left in the United States where people can get off the computer, stop filing tax returns, and in effect become invisible. The rain forests in the Cascades and parts of West Montana come to mind . . . the other place is the Atchafalaya Basin" (*Crusader's Cross* 215). It is significant that western Montana is also named since that is where Burke has made his home in his latter years and also where the novels featuring Robicheaux are increasingly likely to be set in part, with the recent novel *Light of the World* set exclusively in that location. Clearly Burke has at least a grudging respect, or fascination, for such places. *Light of the World* concludes with a scene in which Clete and Robicheaux are reflecting on their lives, debating whether the good in them outweighs the bad, as they hike up a mountain surrounded by "trees so thick and tall on either side of us that they seemed to touch the clouds, more like the pillars of heaven than earthly trees" (548). From this, it can be inferred that Robicheaux has found a new Eden, that even his idealized New Iberia has been sufficiently tarnished by man's intrusion to force him to seek a place for a new beginning. It is also a place where he has just seen evil defeated. There is no mention of an impending return to Louisiana, and readers are left somewhat in the dark at the conclusion of *Light of the World* as to Dave Robicheaux's future.

For the vast majority of the novels, though, it is New Iberia that serves as the main setting, and there are several aspects of the town that Burke highlights as he establishes the place as Robicheaux's hometown. In some novels, Robicheaux describes the town he knew in his youth, and this New Iberia seems to represent much of what was good with the world. Certainly, in such descriptions there is as much attention paid to the ambience as there is to actual landmarks. Toward the conclusion of *Heaven's Prisoners,* while Dave is still dealing with the death of Annie, he describes the "strange things" he did during the last week of August, as the summer is drawing to a close; he includes this memory of visiting Tee Neg's pool hall: "Forty years ago my father and I had come here for a *fais dodo* on July Fourth, and the people had cooked a pig in the ground and drunk wine out of Mason jars and danced to an accordion band on a houseboat until the sun was a red flare on the horizon and the mosquitoes were black on our skin" (273). As he stares out the window of his truck, he observes, "Three blue herons sailed low against the late sun, and with a sinking of the heart I knew that the world in which I had grown up was almost gone and it would not come aborning again" (273). Then, he ponders his adversary, Bubba Rocque, a man with whom he grew up and a man whose wife was behind Annie's death.

> Maybe Bubba Rocque and I had been more alike than I cared to admit. Maybe we both belonged to the past, back there in those green summers of bush-league baseball and crab boils and the smoke of neighborhood fish fries drifting in the trees. Every morning came to you like a strawberry bursting on the tongue. . . . In the heat of the afternoon we sat on the tailgate of the ice wagon at the depot, watching the troop trains roll through town, then fought imaginary wars with stalks of sugarcane, unaware that our little piece of Cajun geography was being consumed on the edges like an old photograph held to a flame. (274)

The New Iberia about which Robicheaux reminisces is lush, green, verdant, promising, sweet, and suggests the naïveté of childhood and the innocence of those who grow up in such an environment. This is the New Iberia that Robicheaux wants to preserve and cling to, because it represents a state of being before corruption of the worst kind entered his world. He realizes, though, that even if he can return there from New Orleans, a city that he associates with corruption and degradation, his own Eden has also been corrupted, perhaps by its proximity to the Big Easy (especially in the years following Hurricane Katrina and the influx of New Orleans residents to Lafayette and surrounding towns), and perhaps by its willingness to allow outside influences to become part of its modern reality.

Often, Robicheaux's memories of New Iberia are tied to memories of his family. In *The Neon Rain*, he is with Annie and craving an alcoholic drink, trying to resist the temptation. They both order a Dr. Pepper and he tries to focus on what is good, telling Annie: "When I was a kid in New Iberia, we had a drink called Dr. Nut. It tasted just like this. . . . My father always bought my brother and me a Dr. Nut when we went to town. That was a big treat back then" (175).

Robicheaux lives the famous observation by Faulkner: "The past is never dead; it isn't even past."[1] Each place in New Iberia seems to co-exist simultaneously in the past and in the present, as though the two cannot be separated. When he visits a poolroom in *Heaven's Prisoners*, he remarks that "the inside of the poolroom was like a partial return into the New Iberia of my youth, when people spoke French more often than English, when there were slot and race-horse machines in every bar, and the cribs on Railroad Avenue stayed open twenty-four hours a day and the rest of the world was as foreign to us as the Texans who arrived after World War II with their oil rigs and pipeline companies" (82). Even though there are elements of this memory that are not so innocent, such as the all-night cribs, a reference to low-rent prostitution, his tone is still one of nostalgia. It is as though anything that happened *inside* his world was safe or at least familiar, while what encroached from the outside was what needed to be both feared and prevented. That change came incrementally, which proved to be the undoing, in Robicheaux's mind, of both his innocence and his town. As he recalls his home, built by his father's own hands, and the childhood spent there, Robicheaux asserts: "Even though my mother died when I was young, and we were poor and my father sometimes brawled in bars and got locked in the parish jail, he and my little brother and I had a home—actually a world—on the bayou that was always safe, warm in the winter from the woodstove, cool in the summer under the shade of the pecan trees, a place that was ours and had belonged to our people and way of life since the Acadians came to Louisiana in 1755" (*Heaven's Prisoners* 45).

Robicheaux's memories, past, and family are all linked to the place and town he called home, and to the past represented by his Cajun ancestors, those who chose Louisiana as home and whose presence now helps to define Dave Robicheaux in his own century. That he specifically mentions the year that the Acadians were expelled by the British from Nova Scotia and forced to disperse to various states along the Eastern Seaboard serves to link Robicheaux strongly to the history not only of his immediate family and community, but of his culture as well. It is the land that provides the link, along with everything that the land represents. They are inextricably connected and cannot be separated, no matter where Robicheaux is. His ancestry, and his history, are a part of his DNA as indelibly as any biological element.

In many ways, New Iberia represents not just itself but many southern towns, especially in an era more innocent than the twenty-first century. Robicheaux makes this connection when, in *A Stained White Radiance,* he talks about growing up in a southern town, not specifically a Louisiana town, and recalls summers spent there, replete with "barbecues and fish fries, the smoke drifting in the oak trees . . . the innocent lust we discovered in convertibles by shadowed lakes groaning with bullfrogs" in a paragraph that also references the scent of lilac and magnolia (65). He is aware, though, of the flip side of this innocent idyll, and acknowledges its existence: "the boys who went nigger-knocking in the little black community of Sunset, who shot people of color with BB guns and marbles fired from slingshots, who threw M-80s onto the galleries of their pitiful homes. They lived in an area of town with unpaved streets, garbage in the backyards, ditches full of mosquitoes and water moccasins from the coulee. Each morning they got up with their loss, their knowledge of who they were, and went to war with the rest of the world" (65).

Robicheaux includes this information not to excuse the actions of those for whom the experience of growing up southern was not so ideal, but to explain how a group such as the Klan can take root and remain supported in the South. Perhaps this is why Robicheaux calls the land he and his neighbors inhabit "our original sin," for which he claims there is "no baptismal rite to expunge it from our lives" since "that green-purple field of new cane was rooted in rib cage and eye socket" (*Burning Angel* 215–16)—that is, planted at the expense of those whose lives were wasted in working it.

He is also aware of the ways in which his world changed after the invasion of the oil companies, a change for which he feels Louisiana had no defense. "Over the years I had seen all the dark players get to southern Louisiana in one form or another: the oil and chemical companies who drained and polluted the wetlands; developers who could turn sugarcane acreage into miles of tract homes and shopping malls that had the aesthetic qualities of a sewer works; and the Mafia who operated out of New Orleans and brought us prostitution, slot machines, control of at least two big labor unions, and finally narcotics" (30). The change that these groups bring to his world is profound and never without considerable cost to an area especially ill prepared to meet the challenges: "They came into an area where large numbers of the people were poor and illiterate, where many were unable to speak English and the politicians were traditionally inept or corrupt, and they took everything that was best from the Cajun world in which I had grown up, treated it cynically and with contempt, and left us with oil sludge in the oyster beds, Levittown, and the abiding knowledge that we had done virtually nothing to stop them" (31).

It is as if Robicheaux sees both himself and his neighbors as complicit in their own destruction and the destruction of their unique way of life, one that was at once both quintessentially southern and uniquely Cajun. His comments about the oil sludge in the oyster beds came before the profound oil spill of 2010 that caused great and lasting damage to the Gulf Coast, and even before Hurricanes Katrina and Rita wrought damage of a different but equally devastating kind to the coast.

It is a theme that Robicheaux returns to frequently—the damage done to both the psychological and environmental nature of the state.

As he describes the journey from Jeanerette, a small town that in many ways represents the New Iberia of his youth, he contrasts his idealization of the place with the present reality: "But inside that perfect bucolic moment, there is another reality at work, one that doesn't stand examination in the harsh light of day. The rain ditches along that same road are strewn with bottles, beer cans, and raw garbage. Under the bayou's rain-dented surface lie discarded paint and motor-oil cans, containers of industrial solvents, rubber tires, and construction debris that will never biologically degrade" (*Crusader's Cross* 38). The contrast continues as he observes: "Across the drawbridge from two of the most lovely historical homes in Louisiana is a trailer slum that probably has no equivalent outside the Third World" (38). However, the reality is one that Robicheaux has no mechanism with which to deal, so "I try not to dwell upon the problems of the era in which we live. I try to remember the Louisiana of my youth and to convince myself that we can rehabilitate the land and ourselves and regain the past. It's a debate which I seldom win" (38).

There is also an irony here in that the "lovely historical homes" represent something of a façade or an illusion. Their loveliness came at the expense of those who toiled to allow a select few to live in such splendor. Burke addresses this irony when he introduces Moleen Bertrand, an example of "old money" in *Burning Angel*: "Moleen Bertrand lived in an enormous white-columned home on Bayou Teche, just east of City Park, and from his glassed-in back porch you could look down the slope of his lawn, through the widely spaced live oak trees, and see the brown current drifting by" (16). He continues, noting that Bertrand "had been born to an exclusionary world of wealth and private schools" (16), and adds that he "never gave offense or was known to be unkind" (16). For all this, though, Bertrand's largesse suggests a type of patriarchal attitude to the descendants of the slaves who worked to provide the home and lifestyle that he has inherited. When Robicheaux confronts him about a claim being made by one of the African American women, Bertha Fontenot, who lives in a cabin on his estate, Bertrand reminds him that there are "six or seven nigra families in there we've taken care of for fifty years. I'm talking about doctor and dentist bills, schooling, extra money for June 'Teenth, getting people out of jail. Bertie tends to forget some things" (17). Like Karyn and Buford LaRose in *Cadillac Jukebox,* who embody the same lifestyle as Bertrand, and who are burned to death in their plantation house, Bertrand meets an unfortunate end in what appears to be a double suicide with his African American mistress, Ruthie-Jean Fontenot (Bertha's daughter). As he ponders the place and method of death, Robicheaux explains: "I believe Moleen Bertrand was like many of my generation with whom I grew up along Bayou Teche. We found ourselves caught inside a historical envelope that we never understood, borne along on wind currents that marked our end, not our beginning, first as remnants of a dying Acadian culture, later as part of that excoriated neo-colonial army who would go off to a war whose origins are as arcane to us as the economics of French poppy growers" (335). Bertrand and his lover end their lives in an apartment on the edge of the French Quarter in New Orleans, a place that Robicheaux describes as "the signature of Moleen's world—jaded, alluring in its decay, seemingly reborn daily amidst the tropical flowers and Gulf rainstorms, inextricably linked to a corrupt past that we secretly admired" (335). Bertrand, and the home that he lives in, one of the "lovely historical homes" that Robicheaux so admires as part of the New Iberia he enjoys, seem to represent the best and worst of Louisiana's past. The deaths of Bertrand and the LaRoses, both by unnatural and violent means, suggest an acknowledgment that the world these homes represent is dying and will ultimately meet with a violent end. It cannot be sustained in the Louisiana embarking on the twenty-first century.

In *Crusader's Cross,* Robicheaux describes New Iberia as always having been an "insular place, Shintoistic, protective of its traditions, virtually incestuous in its familial relationships and attitudes toward outsiders" (152). Neither is it just New Iberia for which, at times, Robicheaux seems to harbor mixed or blended feelings. In *Jolie Blon's Bounce,* he makes the bold announcement that "a love affair with Louisiana is in some ways like falling in love with the biblical whore of Babylon" (177). He clarifies what he means: "We try to smile at its carnival-like politics, its sweaty, whiskey-soaked demagogues, the ignorance bred by its poverty and the insularity of its Cajun and Afro-Caribbean culture. But our self-deprecating manner is a poor disguise for the realities that hover on the edges of one's vision like dirty smudges on a family portrait" (177). The last part of the statement suggests the sense of intimacy and fondness that he feels for his home state, while acknowledging his awareness of both the reality and the attitude that "insiders" have toward the problems that seem to abound.

As in other novels, he then turns attention to the "mind-numbing amounts of litter" that adorn parking lots and roadsides, and attributes it to the "poor and the uneducated and the revelers for whom a self-congratulatory hedonism is a way of life" (177). He calls out the land developers who, overnight, destroy oaks that have stood for two hundred years, and the petrochemical industries that poison waterways, especially those in rural black communities. He concludes, "Rather than fight monied interests, most of the state's politicians give their constituency casinos and Powerball lotteries and drive-by daiquiri windows, along with low income taxes for the wealthy and an eight and one quarter percent sales tax on food for the poor" (177). He is aware that Louisiana has been complicit in its own denouement. When he talks to a priest in New Iberia in *Burning Angel,* the priest understands Robicheaux's desire for the world the past represents, but misunderstands Robicheaux's current mindset. He says to Robicheaux, "It's all this, isn't it? We're still standing in the same space where we grew up but we don't recognize it anymore. It's like other people own it now" (243). He continues: "Dave, when we say the Serenity Prayer about acceptance, we have to mean it. I can absolve sins but I can't set either one of us free from the nature of time" (244). Robicheaux responds: "It has nothing to do with time. It's what we allowed them to do—all of them, the dope traffickers, the industrialists, the politicians. We gave it up without even a fight" (244). This, for Robicheaux, is the greatest tragedy of all. He does not sugarcoat either New Iberia's or Louisiana's past, but presents both sides of the coin: the innocence it once represented for him, and the profound loss of that innocence and the resulting knowledge that always seems to contain its share of pain.

But even though Burke does not shrink from describing New Iberia's drawbacks, his depiction and often celebration of it in the novels has led to interesting developments for the town in terms of tourism. In recent years, the tourist industry has sought to offer more to visitors than mere sights and old buildings. Today's tourists seek as much to experience as to observe. They might visit Savannah, Georgia, and enjoy its historic charm, but it is aspects such as the ability to relate the city to John Berendt's novel *Midnight in the Garden of Good and Evil* and the pleasure of dining at Paula Deen's restaurant that make it more than merely a city of historic interest. The experiential part comes from the interaction between the tourist and the city's offerings. Cultural tourism is an industry that has developed in recent years, along with literary tourism and culinary tourism, both of which can be experienced in a city like Savannah and now, thanks to Dave Robicheaux, New Iberia. In order to experience Robicheaux's hometown, one wants to eat authentically at restaurants and other places mentioned in the novels. Cafeterias and restaurants such as Victor's and Mulate's (in nearby Breaux Bridge) have gotten publicity through Burke's novels. Mulate's is already well known among visitors to the area, while cafeterias such as Victor's have benefited less from their inclusion in the novels.

What the novels have done is to make the town of New Iberia accessible to readers on an emotional level and to connect the town, in readers' minds, with Robicheaux and especially with his childhood and his longing for the past. Burke's readers seem to have little difficulty relating to Robicheaux on an emotional level. His readers often feel a connection with Robicheaux that is also associated with New Iberia. One reader confessed via a third party that she visited New Iberia based solely on what she had read about the town in Burke's books. While there, she mailed a postcard to her home address signed "Dave." She was creating a fantasy for herself based upon her connection with Robicheaux's character and, by extension, his hometown. Her fondness for the character led her to visit his town in order to experience for herself the culture, ambience, and locale with which she had familiarized herself in her reading. Her connection with New

Iberia resided in her emotional connection with Robicheaux, and she embraced the culture as one would the culture of a person with whom one is in a relationship. As mentioned in the introduction, my own visits to the Lafayette/New Iberia area as a graduate student resulted in my moving to Lafayette for six years, absorbing Robicheaux's culture and having my own, albeit less violent, Robicheaux-esque experiences along the way.

Those whose job it is to market the town, and those who could benefit from its marketing, have a distinct advantage over those trying to sell a cultural tourism experience in a town that is not featured in a series of best-selling novels. Barbara Kirshenblatt-Gimblett cites a publication issued by the National Trust for Historic Preservation that stresses the importance of making heritage resources "emotionally accessible"(168).² She insists that sites cannot tell their own story; interpretation is important in "selling" the site and the experience. Like Ellis Island or many Civil War battlefields, the site cannot interpret itself, leading to a flat, emotionless experience without the assistance of interpretation.

New Iberia has been made emotionally accessible by Burke. So deep is the connection between Robicheaux and the readers that they already have a connection with the town, albeit an imaginary one, before they ever set foot there. In fact, many have very distinct ideas of what New Iberia is like without having been there, their impressions having been strongly formed and forged by both Burke's detailed descriptions of the landscape and his skillful inclusion of local landmarks that evoke the culture and the people about which he writes. The area has received even more publicity of late since it was chosen as the first setting for the HBO series *True Detective*. A recent article describes how viewers of the series travel to the towns featured to see landmarks from the shows. Like Burke, the show's creators chose as their settings not the more obvious New Orleans but small southwestern Louisiana towns like Erath, Carencro, and Opelousas. The writer of the article was less than impressed: "Just think, these people are [sic] traveled hundreds of miles to see what? An unassuming oak tree that served as a show murder scene? A snoball stand where the characters

Rust Cohle and Marty Hart, portrayed by [Matthew] McConaughey and Woody Harrelson, argued about the meaning of life? A bungalow painted an unfortunate shade of green? This couldn't be enough for them, right?" She continues, "It was enough" (Banner).

Burke's choice of New Iberia as the setting for many of his Robicheaux novels has had consequences for the town that few, including Burke, could have predicted. He admits that he had "no idea" how popular his books would be, nor did he suspect how much attention they would draw to the town he grew up in (telephone interview, November 12, 2002). Although not born in New Iberia (he was born in Texas), Burke grew up in a house along the banks of the Bayou Teche, much like Robicheaux. If his depiction of the town and the culture is occasionally influenced more by popular opinion and stereotyping than by fact, he nonetheless writes with authority about his hometown and imbues Robicheaux with the same affection for the town that he himself undoubtedly possesses.

Ostensibly, Burke sets his Robicheaux novels in the present, but much of the past seeps into the stories. The case could even be made that the New Iberia about which he writes is a town of the past, before the "invasion" of McDonald's, Wal-Mart, and other features of Anytown, USA, together with a few details unique to the area such as the drive-through daiquiri stands. In an article for England's *Telegraph* magazine, writer John Williams states, "If you come to Louisiana looking for the world depicted in Burke's books you might find it hard to find, because Burke's Louisiana is a strange, often almost hallucinatory mixture of the past and present" (56). Robicheaux acknowledges this aspect of his connection to New Iberia when he describes a scene in *Jolie Blon's Bounce* as he drives down East Main: "I parked by the Shadows, where a tourist bus was unloading, and crossed the street and entered a two-story Victorian house that had been remodeled into the law offices of Perry LaSalle. It was like entering a monument to the past" (140). Robicheaux accepts that elements of the town are not only linked to the past, but retain vestiges of the past, and this is an element that features strongly in Burke's descriptions of the town. As a writer, Burke has the privilege of writing a town or place the way that he would like it to be. Certainly, he does not whitewash New Iberia's past or its faults, but he also emphasizes what is appealing: the sense of community, the people, the food, the music, and, good or bad, the strong ties to the past and a sense of a shared history.

As interest in New Iberia grew in the minds of Burke's readers, there were bound to be preconceived ideas fueled by the picture Burke paints. Some readers who began to visit the town needed a way of connecting the mental image they had with the reality. How were they to know what was fact and what fiction? Was St. Peter's Church real? Del's? Shadows on the Teche? How about Victor's Cafeteria? As people began to visit Books along the Teche, the locally owned bookstore and scene of many book signings by Burke, and to ask questions about Robicheaux's hometown, the line between what was real and what was fiction became increasingly blurred. Robicheaux's boat and bait business was of particular interest but, of course, does not exist in reality. However, readers can purchase a T-shirt advertising the business on Burke's own website. Other items are available, all linking the reader to the Robicheaux experience. Those wishing to experience the "real thing" can visit iberiatravel.com, where a click of the mouse will take them to a page about the town's favorite author. It describes New Iberia as a "fascinating blend of heritage, hospitality, and history" and includes a link to a brief video explaining Burke's connection to the area. Included is Robicheaux's description of the town's Main Street from *A Stained White Radiance,* ending with the comment that the scene "looks like a postcard mailed from the nineteenth century." It is interesting that it is again a scene from the past that is referenced, since so much of Robicheaux's affection for the town is inextricably linked to his affection for the past. The website also acknowledges that Burke now lives in Missoula, Montana, a fact the reader of the recent novel *Light of the World* might have inferred.

Although previous novels featuring Robicheaux have been partially set in Missoula (*Black Cherry Blues* is set almost exclusively there), *Light of the World* is the first novel that takes place there from start to finish. The main characters are the same: his childhood friend, former partner, and longtime sidekick Clete Purcel; his daughter, Alafair; and Clete's daughter, Gretchen. But the setting is decidedly different. As would be expected, Montana and its scenery are beautifully described by Burke. And, while many readers link Robicheaux with Burke himself, the character with whom Robicheaux and Alafair are visiting in this novel sounds a lot like Burke. He describes Albert Hollister as "a novelist and retired English professor" (7), then describes his home as a place "where Albert could continue to wage war against the intrusions of the Industrial Age" (7). The same passage also references Hollister's Asian wife, another aspect of his life that Burke shares. In this novel, although Robicheaux is away from New Iberia, it seems that New Iberia is never far away from him. When reminiscing about Alafair's childhood, he talks of "when we lived in an idyllic world south of New Iberia" (351). And, when talking with Clete, he "thought of all the days Clete and I had hiked through woods to get to an isolated pond in the Atchafalaya Basin. I thought about diving the wreck of German sub that drifted up and down the Louisiana coast, and knocking down ducks inside a blind on Whiskey Bay" (442). To adapt an old adage, "You can take the boy out of Louisiana, but you can't take Louisiana out of the boy."

It could be said, though, that it is New Orleans that is more strongly representative of the past for Robicheaux in this novel, given Clete's relationship with New Orleans native Felicity Louviere. Robicheaux goes into some detail describing the city, including its unique dialect: "'New Orleans' was pronounced as 'New Or Lons' and never, under any circumstances, not even at gunpoint, 'Nawlens'" (198) and explaining that the dialect sounded more like Brooklyn than the South. He also explains Clete and Felicity's affinity for each other as coming from the fact that "we both grew up in the same part of New Orleans. Because everybody from Uptown knows what everybody else there is thinking. It's probably like an A.A. meeting. There's only one story in the room. We all come out of the same culture" (205). This agrees with opinions expressed by Chris Wiltz's Neal Rafferty, who also makes a point of distinguishing between the different neighborhoods of New Orleans. In a scene from *The Emerald Lizard*, Rafferty explains: "I'm a good New Orleans boy, so I'll admit to a certain prejudice against

New Iberia

the West Bank. You know, sort of an 'Our team is the best team' attitude. But I grew up in the Irish Channel, and a lot of people on the other side of Magazine Street were told not to associate with anyone from the Channel" (25). Rafferty concedes, though, "In the end we're all from the same hot bayou country" (25), perhaps the point that Robicheaux is also trying to make.

If New Iberia has become associated with Robicheaux's roots not only as a setting but as an integral part of the novels, is Robicheaux still Robicheaux when set down in another part of the country, albeit one that also allows for folk justice and other less-regulated aspects of the Louisiana experience? Is Robicheaux the same when away from the live oaks and the gumbo and the music that have informed his experience and helped mold him into the man he has become? Only readers can decide that, but at the conclusion of *Light of the World*, I personally longed for him to pack up and return to New Iberia. Even if he can relocate, I'm not sure that his readers can! There may, though, be an explanation for the move both simpler and more profound than can be surmised. Burke's own explanation, provided in an e-mail, is that the series of Robicheaux novels begins with a trilogy that ends in Montana (*The Neon Rain*, *Heaven's Prisoners*, and *Black Cherry Blues*), and the twenty novels conclude with a trilogy that also ends in Montana (*The Glass Rainbow*, *Creole Belle*, and *Light of the World*).[3] In the same e-mail he explains, "I started out with Milton in mind, and ended with him." He then modestly adds, "I think he's pretty good company, although I don't rank my work with his." Whether or not readers are familiar with Milton's works and his depiction of the struggle between good and evil, a familiar theme in Burke's books, there is a deliberate pattern to the way in which Burke presents his works that allows Robicheaux to function as a champion for good in either location. Readers will have to make up their own minds as to what they think about the change in location, given their connection to Robicheaux and the place he called home for so many years.

Even while acknowledging New Iberia's shortcomings, its change over time, and its sometimes volatile history, Robicheaux allows his affection for his hometown to shine through. This is true of everything and everyone else he holds dear. Much as he is aware and even critical of areas of Clete's life, his devotion to Clete is obvious. It is the same with New Iberia and much of his home state of Louisiana. Clearly, there is more to love than to dislike, and more that holds fond memories than that repels. For all its faults, New Iberia is and probably will ever be home, at least in the minds of Burke's readers.

CONCLUSION
THE ROOTS RUN DEEP

There are many ways that an author can create a sense of place. Writers of detective fiction such as Hillerman and Parker, who chose non-Louisiana settings for their novels, created a sense of place through examples of the local geography and tradition (Fenway Park, the Charles River, MIT in Parker's case; extravagant descriptions of both the geography and the Navajo culture in Hillerman's case). Other writers of detective fiction such as Smith and Wiltz, who write a specifically Louisiana type of novel, focus on New Orleans, Louisiana's best-known city, by including examples of both the landscape and the culture. Utilizing the reader's senses, emphasizing perhaps local foodways such as coffee and beignets, helps these writers create a New Orleans atmosphere.

Sometimes a connection between the reader and the setting is not important. The story being told could take place anywhere, and it would not suffer from the lack of such a connection. For James Lee Burke, though, the setting might have been incidental at the outset, but it has become an integral part of the Robicheaux novels because it is an integral part of Robicheaux, both in terms of his development as a character and in terms of creating a sense of connection between readers and the character they think of as Dave, a man they would like to have as a friend, ally, or possibly lover. He is as real to them as a favorite character on a television show, possibly more so since the physical presence of the person can be left to the imagination. Readers do not know Robicheaux's height, or his weight. His black hair is streaked with white from the malnutrition he experienced growing up and may by now be streaked with gray also. But much of his appearance is left to the imagination, perhaps because the novels are narrated in the first person and Robicheaux is more likely to obsess over his internal condition than the external. His background and upbringing, however, his family and cultural roots, are very vividly shared with the reader, and this allows, perhaps almost guarantees, that reading more than one novel will begin to create a sense of shared intimacy between the reader and the character. We begin to feel as though we know Robicheaux. We know where he will eat lunch, what he will eat, the kind of leisure activities he enjoys (crawfish boils, jogging, exercising, listening to a Cajun band at an open air festival), and we know how he will react in a given circumstance. When someone "pushes his buttons," we hold our breath wondering how far Robicheaux will go this time. We know the situations that will push him toward his main weakness, alcohol, and we know what will pull him back. We know the church he attends and the library where Alafair meets her friends to study for classes. We also know how he feels about modern intrusions like Wal-Mart, fast-food restaurants, casinos, and drive-through daiquiri stands, as well as the influx of people whose intentions toward his hometown and his state might not be honorable nor beneficial to those whose past and future are as connected to the area as he is.

Over time, just as the details we know about a friend accumulate as we spend more time with them, we begin to "know" Robicheaux. We know, because Burke draws a meticulous picture of the landscape, the history, and the culture that have nurtured Robicheaux. We know that his family has strong ties to the land, going back to the Civil War and beyond. We know that his father's connection to the land continues, in spite of his father's death, when Robicheaux describes scenes that he shared with his father, both in life and in death. And it is in these supernatural moments, when Robicheaux is convinced that both his father and Annie still communicate with him through the moisture-drenched Louisiana atmosphere, that readers have perhaps their greatest connection with Robicheaux, a man for whom love conquers even death.

Conclusion

This connection is not coincidental. It has been carefully crafted by Burke as he reveals more and more about Robicheaux as time and the novels progress. Through the thoughtful and careful inclusion of such details as the description of New Iberia's Main Street and of the Atchafalaya Basin, and through the use of language and dialect, he sets the scene and allows readers into Robicheaux's private world. Burke shares a conversation between Robicheaux and a childhood friend or with Batist without feeling the need to interpret the literal meaning of the conversation (that might be considered patronizing since we are, after all, a part of Robicheaux's world, too), but always implying it. It is in the folk sayings, the adages and pieces of advice passed on from father to son, that we learn more about local wildlife, the attitude toward authority figures, and the logical way to go about solving a problem.

The inclusion of a musical score takes not only Robicheaux back to the New Iberia of his childhood and adolescence. It takes us along with him, as though we too can understand what it was like to grow up in a small Louisiana town before the civil rights movement. The music also alludes to falling in love, not only perhaps with his first romantic love (Bootsie Mouton, who later became his third wife), but also with his hometown, with his culture, and with a heritage unique to that part of the country. It might not be a revelation, but the love affair begins to take root and, as with any love that stands the test of time, grows deeper and stronger like the roots of the live oaks that line Main Street. That much of the music is specific to his Cajun upbringing is not coincidental. That "La Jolie Blond" refers to a poignant lost love is also not coincidental. The time it represents is also lost, and readers understand that the time and place epitomized by this song are the same time and place in which Robicheaux would like to have remained forever.

The Robicheaux that readers have come to know is not merely a detective, but a Cajun detective who still cooks the recipes taught to him by his father, still maintains a close relationship with his father's friend and employee, Batist, and still wants to believe the best of his mother. He still wants to be able to walk (or jog) Main Street and not be confronted with the big box stores that have desecrated and decimated the main streets of many small towns. He wants to be able to share iced tea with a neighbor, and to keep his daughter's pet raccoon safe from predators. Who he is is so closely connected with his hometown and with the culture represented by that hometown that the two cannot be separated, even with increasingly lengthy and specific forays into Montana.

Robicheaux's past and present are so closely linked that the two are inseparable, another aspect of the novels that makes them distinct and likely to stand the test of time. Readers can be told about Aldous not only as a figure from Dave's past, but also as a figure from his present, one who returns in times of crisis and serves to establish Robicheaux's connection to his roots. For Robicheaux, the connection is deep, profound, and personal, and it is this aspect of his personality that makes Dave Robicheaux an unforgettable and accessible character, one that readers will want to reconnect with. As readers visit the novels time and time again (as Burke's readers have a tendency to do), it is my desire that a deeper understanding and appreciation of the culture about which Burke writes will create a deeper connection with Robicheaux, a character who will, undoubtedly, share his life and his hometown with readers for many generations to come.

NOTES

INTRODUCTION

1. To clarify, *Cajun* refers to the descendants of settlers of French heritage who inhabited the Nova Scotia region of Canada and were expelled by the British in 1755. After unsuccessfully trying to put down roots at various places along the Eastern Seaboard, many eventually wound up in Louisiana, a place where their Catholic faith did not make them unwelcome. The term *Creole* is less easily defined since its meaning has changed over time. Originally referring to someone of European descent born in the United States (often of French or Spanish heritage, and often a first-generation immigrant), it now commonly refers to someone of African American heritage or of mixed racial heritage.

1. LANGUAGE, DIALECT, AND FOLK SAYINGS

1. An idea discussed by Ancelet, Edwards, and Pitre in *Cajun Country*.
2. Code switching is the ability to change from one language or dialect to another as the occasion demands it, as put forth by Wardhaugh in *An Introduction to Sociolinguistics*.
3. Levine provides information on this idea in *Black Culture and Black Consciousness*.

2. THE SOUNDTRACK OF A CULTURE

1. In his book *Swamp Pop*, Bernard goes into the origins of this uniquely Louisiana style of music.
2. Ancelet, Edwards, and Pitre detail the development of Cajun music in *Cajun Country*.
3. More detailed information on this song, and others, can be found in Gaudet's *Tales from the Levee*.

3. ROBICHEAUX'S ROUX

1. The concept of foodways includes not only the type of food being presented but also elements of its preparation and serving, together with its connection to and association with the local environment and culture. Gutierrez, in *Cajun Foodways*, explicitly looks at many aspects of food, its presentation, its connection to the people, and the role of performance in its preparation and delivery.

2. Kalčik's essay "Ethnic Foodways in America" emphasizes the importance of food as a part of cultural identity.

3. In the early days of settlement of Acadiana, there were many contributions from Native Americans that helped the Cajun newcomers survive in a place that differed from what they were accustomed to not only in climate, but also in types of foods, landscape, and many other aspects that make Louisiana unique.

4. It is significant that Wiltz mentions the environmental impact of the redfish industry since the impact on Louisiana's environment of all kinds of industries is a subject near and dear to Robicheaux's heart and is often addressed in Burke's novels.

5. Bienvenu's classic cookbook of south Louisiana recipes has the memorable title *Who's Your Mama, Are You Catholic, and Can You Make a Roux?*—referring, tongue-in-cheek, to questions commonly asked by residents to establish a person's connection to the area.

6. Roux is the base for other signature dishes of Louisiana as well, such as étouffée and sauce piquante.

7. Hill's essay "'Use to, the Menfolks Would Eat First'" discusses what she terms "food rituals" as an aspect of foodways dealing with the serving and presenting of food as much as the food itself—an idea also incorporated into Burke's writing.

8. This point was confirmed for me by Louisiana native and Cajun folklorist Barry Jean Ancelet.

4. BELIEFS ALONG THE BAYOU

1. Hufford's work on what he terms "unofficial beliefs" needs to be mentioned, in particular "Beings without Bodies: An Experience-Centered Theory of the Belief in Spirits." Hufford is commonly credited with delineating the difference between "official" and "unofficial" beliefs.

2. Levine's *Black Culture and Black Consciousness* addresses such issues and is an excellent source for further study.

3. This story, "Love," can be found in Butler's collection *A Good Scent from a Strange Mountain*.

5. SOMETHING IN THE WATER

1. Honko describes and discusses von Sydow's idea in her article "Memorates and the Study of Folk Beliefs."

2. Even though Bennett's article, "Heavenly Protection and Family Unity: The Concept of the Revenant among Elderly Urban Women," refers to a study among a specific community in England, her ideas are applicable to Burke's with regard to the revenant, especially as to specific details of the function of the revenant.

3. Jan Harold Brunvand can be credited with bringing the term *revenant* into wide use among scholars of such phenomena.

4. Burke talks about this in an interview conducted by the Catholic network EWTN in its program *The World Over*.

5. Burke's use of the name Legion here is clearly a reference to the biblical story of the healing of a demon-possessed man by Jesus. Jesus confronts the man, asking, "What is your name?" The man responds, "My name is Legion . . . for we are many" (Mark 5:1–13, New International Version).

6. FIGHTING THE GOOD FIGHT

1. Cawelti's study *Adventure, Mystery, and Romance* discusses the attributes associated with hard-boiled detective fiction, a description that tends to be met in Robicheaux and the type of adventures in which Burke embroils him.

2. Reed's work on southern culture, and on southern violence in particular, in his essay "Below the Smith and Wesson Line" (in *One South*) helps explain how Burke writes incidents of violence that might well be considered too graphic if taken out of the context of both a southern setting and the genre of detective fiction in which he is writing.

3. Montell, whose studies are also about incidents in the South, seems to confirm the findings of Reed.

7. NEW IBERIA

1. Perhaps Faulkner's best-known line, taken from his play *Requiem for a Nun*, it seems to apply to the majority of what can be termed "southern fiction."

2. Kirshenblatt-Gimblett's work *Destination Culture* notes the link in recent popular tourism between culture and place, something that New Iberia has incorporated into its own marketing since Burke has made the town popular through his writing.

3. Burke was kind enough to share this information in an e-mail. His willingness to reply to my inquiry is greatly appreciated.

BIBLIOGRAPHY

BOOKS AND ARTICLES

Ancelet, Barry Jean. "Cajun and Zydeco Music Traditions." Folklife in Louisiana website, accessed December 15, 2015.

———. "Lomax in Louisiana: Trials and Triumph." Folklife in Louisiana website, accessed December 21, 2015.

Ancelet, Barry Jean, Jay Edwards, and Glen Pitre. *Cajun Country.* Jackson: University Press of Mississippi, 1991.

Banner, Jo. "Seven True Detective Filming Locations to Visit." http://www.Louisianatravel.com/blog/7-true-detective-filming-locations-visit, accessed December 9, 2015.

Bennett, Gillian. "Heavenly Protection and Family Unity: The Concept of the Revenant among Elderly Urban Women." *Folklore* 96.1 (1985): 87–97.

Bernard, Shane K. *Swamp Pop: Cajun and Creole Rhythm and Blues.* Jackson: University Press of Mississippi, 1996.

Bienvenu, Marcelle. *Who's Your Mama, Are You Catholic, and Can You Make a Roux? A Family Album Cookbook.* Lafayette: Times of Acadiana Press, 1991.

Brasseaux, Carl (text), and Philip Gould (photographs). *Acadiana: Louisiana's Historic Cajun Country.* Baton Rouge: Louisiana State University Press, 2011.

Brunvand, Jan Harold. *The Study of American Folklore.* New York: W. W. Norton, 1986.

Burke, James Lee. *Black Cherry Blues.* New York: Avon, 1989.

———. *Burning Angel.* New York: Hyperion, 1995.

———. *Cadillac Jukebox*. New York: Hyperion, 1996.
———. *Creole Belle*. New York: Simon and Schuster, 2012.
———. *Crusader's Cross*. New York: Simon and Schuster, 2005.
———. *Dixie City Jam*. New York: Hyperion, 1994.
———. *Heaven's Prisoners*. New York: Pocket, 1988.
———. *In the Electric Mist with Confederate Dead*. New York: Avon, 1993.
———. *Jolie Blon's Bounce*. New York: Simon and Schuster, 2002.
———. *Last Car to Elysian Fields*. New York: Simon and Schuster, 2003.
———. *Light of the World*. New York: Simon and Schuster, 2013.
———. *A Morning for Flamingos*. New York: Avon, 1990.
———. *The Neon Rain*. New York: Pocket, 1987.
———. *Pegasus Descending*. New York: Simon and Schuster, 2006.
———. *Purple Cane Road*. New York: Dell, 2000.
———. *A Stained White Radiance*. New York: Avon, 1992.
———. *Sunset Limited*. New York: Doubleday, 1998.
Butler, Robert Olen. "Love." In *A Good Scent from a Strange Mountain*. New York: Grove Press, 1992.
Cawelti, John. *Adventure, Mystery, and Romance: Formula Stories as Art and Popular Culture*. Chicago: University of Chicago Press, 1976.
Chopin, Kate. "In Sabine." In *Lilacs and Other Stories*. New York: Dover, 2005.
Faulkner, William. *Requiem for a Nun*. New York: Random House, 1950.
Gaines, Ernest. *A Gathering of Old Men*. New York: Knopf, 1983.
Gaudet, Marcia G. *Tales from the Levee: The Folklore of St. John the Baptist Parish*. Lafayette: Center for Louisiana Studies, University of Southwestern Louisiana, 1984.
Gautreaux, Tim. *Same Place, Same Things*. New York: Picador, 1996.
———. *Welding with Children*. New York: Picador, 2009.
Gutierrez, C. Paige. *Cajun Foodways*. Jackson: University Press of Mississippi, 1992.
Hill, Darlene Reimers. "'Use to, the Menfolks Would Eat First': Food and Food Rituals in the Fiction of Bobbie Ann Mason." *Southern Quarterly* 30 (1992): 81–89.
Hillerman, Tony. *Dance Hall of the Dead*. New York: Harper-Collins, 1973.
Honko, Lauri. "Memorates and the Study of Folk Beliefs." *Journal of the Folklore Institute* 1, no. 1/2 (1964): 5–19.
Hufford, David. "Beings without Bodies: An Experience-Centered Theory

of the Belief in Spirits." In *Out of the Ordinary: Folklore and the Supernatural*, edited by Barbara Walker, 11–45. Logan: Utah State University Press, 1995.

Kalčik, Susan. "Ethnic Foodways in America: Symbol and the Performance of Identity." In *Ethnic and Regional Foodways in the United States: The Performance of Group Identity*, edited by Linda Keller Brown and Kay Mussell, 37–65. Knoxville: University of Tennessee Press, 1984.

Kirshenblatt-Gimblett, Barbara. *Destination Culture: Tourism, Museums, and Heritage*. Berkeley: University of California Press, 1998.

Levine, Lawrence W. *Black Culture and Black Consciousness: Afro-American Folk Thought from Slavery to Freedom*. Oxford: Oxford University Press, 1977.

Montell, William Lynwood. *Killings: Folk Justice in the Upper South*. Lexington: University Press of Kentucky, 1986.

Reed, John Shelton. *One South: An Ethnic Approach to Regional Culture*. Baton Rouge: Louisiana State University Press, 1986.

Richardson, Maggie Heyn. *Hungry for Louisiana: An Omnivore's Journey*. Baton Rouge: Louisiana State University Press, 2015.

Smith, Julie. *Crescent City Kill*. New York: Ballantine, 1997.

Wardhaugh, Ronald. *An Introduction to Sociolinguistics*. Malden, Mass.: Blackwell, 1986.

Williams, John. "Bayou Tapestry." *Telegraph*, June 2, 2001, 52–56.

Wiltz, Chris. *The Emerald Lizard*. New York: Penguin Books, 1991.

MOVIES

The Big Easy. Columbia Pictures, 1987.
No Mercy. TriStar Pictures, 1986.
Passion Fish. Miramax Films, 1992.
Southern Comfort. 20th Century Fox, 1981.

OTHER

Burke, James Lee. Telephone interview, November 12, 2002.
Burke, James Lee. E-mail, August 17, 2015.

INDEX

Note: "Robicheaux" refers to Dave Robicheaux, Burke's central character.

Abshire, Nathan, 37
Acadiana: and belief systems, 66, 67, 69, 76; and Cajun foodways, 26, 55, 57, 92, 138*n*3; and Cajun music, 37, 41; Catholicism in, 93; folk justice in, 104–5; isolation of, 9, 15, 21, 37, 104; New Iberia as Cajun town of, 5; Robicheaux's place in, 121; settlement of, 121; and supernatural experiences, 99–100; water environment of, 92
African Americans: blues music reflecting experiences of, 49, 52; and Creole French, 19–20; culture of, 36, 40, 42; and musical genres, 11, 36, 40, 42, 46; and Robicheaux's acknowledgment of racial differences, 13–14, 121–22; violence toward, 108, 121–22; and voodoo, 67, 69–70, 72
alcohol abuse: Robicheaux's association of zydeco with drinking days, 36, 42, 44; and Robicheaux's attitude toward violence, 109; Robicheaux's history of, 2, 3, 9, 46, 120, 134; and Robicheaux's reaction to murder of Annie, 28, 81–82; and Robicheaux's supernatural experiences, 78, 81–82, 84, 85, 89
Alcoholics Anonymous (AA), 69, 82, 130
alligators, 13, 26–27, 29, 33, 56
Ancelet, Barry Jean, 41, 46, 104, 105, 138*n*8

"Angel of Work Camp Number Nine, The" (song), 51–52
Angola (Louisiana State Penitentiary), 31, 46, 48, 49, 50, 51
animals: of Cajun culture, 13; in Cajun foodways, 34, 56; in folk sayings, 26–27, 29, 34
Appalachian terms, 19
Ardoin, Amédé, 50
armadillos, 13, 27, 56
assimilation, 21, 25, 41
Atchafalaya Basin: and Burke's development of sense of place, 135; and Cajun music, 35; crawfish in, 58; New Iberia distinguished from, 113, 114, 115; Robicheaux's description of, 117–18, 130; and water imagery, 92, 98

baby boomer generation, 14
barbecue, 39, 60–61, 121
Basinger, Kim, 115
Baton Rouge, La., 114
Bayou Teche, 6, 116, 117, 124, 128
Beausoleil (music group), 8, 15
belief systems: and Acadiana, 66, 67, 69, 76; of Batist Perry, 69–70, 75, 99; and coexisting beliefs, 11–12, 66–67, 70–71, 72, 73, 75–76, 77, 100; complexity of, 65, 66, 75–76; and folk beliefs in Burke's novels, 11–12, 65–66, 67, 71, 73,

145

Index

belief systems (*continued*)
74–76, 77, 99–100; and Robicheaux's pragmatism, 65, 67, 68, 71, 73, 74, 100; and Robicheaux's relationship with Bootsie, 70; and Robicheaux's supernatural experiences, 12, 67, 77–80, 82, 84, 86, 88, 89, 99, 100, 134; and Robicheaux's view of water, 93;; and traditional beliefs, 6; and traiteurs, 12, 23, 42–43, 66, 67–68, 70–71, 72, 75, 76, 77; and unofficial beliefs, 66, 138n1
Bennett, Gillian, 78–79, 80, 82, 84, 87, 92, 99, 139n2
Berendt, John, 126
Bernard, Shane, 37, 137n1
Bienvenu, Marcelle, 138n5
Big Easy, The (film), 8, 115
Black Cherry Blues (Burke): and Alafair using English, 20; Alafair's well-being threatened in, 107, 109; Aldous's communication with Robicheaux in, 80–81, 83, 96; Annie's communication with Robicheaux in, 80, 81–84; and Batist Perry's belief systems, 75; blues music in, 47–48; "La Jolie Blonde" in, 38; locally produced music permeating, 36, 42, 53; Montana as setting of portions of story, 129, 131; Purcel's views of violence in, 110; and Robicheaux coping with death of Annie, 47–48, 53, 80, 83, 84; Robicheaux's appreciation of Cajun French in, 20; Robicheaux's attitude toward justice system in, 107; Robicheaux's attitude toward violence in, 109–10; Robicheaux's character in, 2; and Robicheaux's first wife, 32–33; Robicheaux's supernatural experiences in, 80–84, 96
blackened redfish, 59
blues music: African Americans' experiences reflected in, 49, 52; and Creoles, 46; Robicheaux's associations with, 46–50, 54; role in Burke's novels, 36, 40, 46, 51–52
Books along the Teche, New Iberia, 129
Boston, Mass., 3, 114
boudin, 11, 39, 42, 58–59, 63

Breaux Bridge, La., 11, 61–62, 70, 126
Breaux Bridge Crawfish Festival, 57
Brown, Gatemouth, 47
Brunvand, Jan, 78, 139n3
Burke, James Lee: authenticity of writing, 7; Cajun culture in novels of, 1–3, 4, 6, 7, 10, 14–16; childhood of, 6–7; Montana residence of, 8, 116, 118, 129; popularity of Robicheaux novels, 116, 128; Robicheaux's character linked with, 130; and southern fiction genre, 3, 102, 110, 112, 139n2; and theme of struggle between good and evil, 131. *See also specific novels*
Burke, Pierre, 6
Burke, Roberta, 6, 7
Burning Angel (Burke): and belief systems, 73; and Cajun foodways, 62, 63; Purcel's and Marsallus's questionable status, 89–90, 91; and racial distinctions, 31; Robicheaux's description of Louisiana in, 125; Robicheaux's description of race relations in, 123–24; Robicheaux's description of South in, 122; and Robicheaux's ethics regarding violence, 106; and Robicheaux's relationship with Bootsie, 106; and Robicheaux's supernatural experiences, 79, 80, 89–90, 96, 98; and water imagery, 98
Butler, Robert Olen, 71–72, 138n3

Cadillac Jukebox (Burke): Batist Perry on music in, 46; Batist Perry's dialect in, 24–25, 29; Batist Perry's folk sayings in, 29; Cajun foodways in, 60–61; folk sayings in, 29; French language in, 24–25; popular music of region featured in, 36–38, 39, 46; Purcel eating barbecue lunch in, 60; Robicheaux's description of race relations in, 124
Cajun culture: Aldous's embodiment of, 28, 33, 134; and Bootsie, 32; in Burke's novels, 1–3, 4, 6, 7, 10, 14–16; durability of, 28; in film, 8–9, 10, 115–16; importance of oral tradition in, 33; perceptions of, 2, 5, 8–9, 10; popular-

Index

ity of, 114–15; Robicheaux's embodiment of, 1–3, 4, 6, 7, 10, 25, 34, 64, 134; Robicheaux's experience of tensions between cultures, 9, 40; Robicheaux's identification with, 11, 64; and Robicheaux's marriage to Annie, 10, 11, 32, 33; and Robicheaux's relationship with Alafair, 10, 32–33, 62, 134, 136; self-representation of writers within, 9; stereotypes of Cajuns, 8, 10, 17, 33, 55, 63. *See also* belief systems

Cajun foodways: and Acadiana, 26, 55, 57, 92, 138n3; and Batist Perry, 58; and Cajun music, 39, 42, 55, 64; in film, 115; and gender roles, 60; and insider/outsider status, 58–59, 61; and outdoor preparation and eating, 60–61; Prudhomme's introduction of, 8, 15, 57; Robicheaux's learning to cook from Aldous, 56, 60, 61; and Robicheaux's marriage to Annie, 11, 39, 60; role in Burke's novels, 10–11, 34, 55, 56, 58, 61–63, 64, 134, 135, 138n1, 138n7; role of performance in, 57, 60, 138n1; role of water in, 92. *See also specific foods*

Cajun French: Aldous using, 14, 25, 26–27, 31, 80; Burke's use of, 2, 17, 19, 21–22, 30, 31–32; and Cajun foodways, 62; Creole French distinguished from, 20, 22; and folk sayings, 26–27; fragmentation in use of, 32; in New Iberia, 6; and Robicheaux's ties to past, 18, 30–32, 33; and ties to European past, 18

Cajun music: and Beausoleil, 8, 15; and Cajun foodways, 39, 42, 55, 64; in film, 115; and French language, 41; in New Iberia, 6; popularity in Louisiana, 35; Robicheaux's experiences of, 11, 36, 44; and Robicheaux's marriage to Annie, 39; and Robicheaux's relationship with Alafair, 39; and Robicheaux's relationship with Bootsie, 135; role in Burke's novels, 10, 11, 34, 36, 40–41, 44, 52, 134; style of dance associated with, 44–45; and zydeco, 40–41, 45. *See also* "Jolie Blonde, La" (song)

Cajun people: defining of, 137n1; French language identifying, 20, 21, 25–26; historic connection with French culture, 17, 32; stereotypes of, 8, 10, 17, 33, 55, 63

Cash, Johnny, 48

Catholicism: in New Orleans, 72; as predominant religion in Acadiana, 66, 67, 69; and Robicheaux's attitude toward violence, 109; Robicheaux's belief in, 11–12, 68–69, 77, 82, 90; and traiteurs, 70–71; use of water in, 93; voodoo combining African religion with elements of, 67, 72

Cawelti, John, 101–2, 139n1

Chenier, Clifton, 44

Chesnutt, Charles, 71

Choates, Harry, 37–38

Chopin, Kate, 2, 9, 18–19

Civil War, 7, 114, 134

Clanton, Jimmy, 37, 53–54

code switching, 23–24, 137n2

CODOFIL (Council for the Development of French in Louisiana), 14

conjure, and folk beliefs, 65, 71–76

Cops (television show), 4

cracklings (fried pork skin), 62, 63

crawfish: Aldous's story about, 26, 33; in Cajun culture, 13; and Cajun foodways, 2, 11, 15, 34, 39, 55, 56, 57; crawfish boils, 11, 15, 39, 42, 55, 58, 60, 134; in étouffée, 58; in folk sayings, 13, 26

Creole Belle (Burke): Cajun French in, 31–32; Cajun music in, 52–53; Purcel hearing music in, 53; Purcel's views of violence in, 101; Purcel's warning to Robicheaux in, 95–96; and Robicheaux's memories of his parents, 95–96; and Robicheaux's relationship with Alafair, 95; and Robicheaux's use of violence, 101; swamp pop in, 53; as trilogy, 131

Creole French: Batist Perry's use of, 19–20; Burke's use of, 17, 19–22; Cajun French distinguished from, 20, 22; Chopin's use of, 19

Creoles: belief systems of, 66, 75; de-

147

Index

Creoles (*continued*)
  fining of, 137n1; and gumbo, 62; and jambalaya, 56; juré as shout and ring dance tradition of, 41–42; and musical genres, 11, 36, 40, 43, 46
Crusader's Cross (Burke): French language in, 28; "La Jolie Blonde" in, 38; Robicheaux's description of Atchafalaya Basin in, 118; Robicheaux's description of Louisiana in, 123; Robicheaux's description of New Iberia in, 124
curanderas/os, 70–71

dance halls, 35, 105
Deen, Paula, 126
detective fiction: Burke's use of Cajun culture in, 15; flawed detective concept in, 1; hard-boiled detective in, 101–2, 112, 139n1; Robicheaux as Cajun detective, 25; Robicheaux as hard-boiled detective, 101, 112, 139n1; settings of, 3–4, 5, 133; violence in, 139n2
dialects: Annie's understanding of, 22, 25; Batist Perry's dialect, 20, 22–25, 29, 31, 135; Burke's interspersing standard English with other dialects, 14, 18, 22–23; Burke's use of, 13, 17–18, 21–22, 33, 135; Chopin's use of, 18–19; and folk sayings, 29; Robicheaux's experiences with, 22, 130; and Robicheaux's supernatural experiences, 80
Dixie City Jam (Burke): and Batist Perry's belief systems, 69–70; description of Batist Perry in, 13; Nazi submarine in, 7; popular music referred to, 37; Robicheaux's belief system in, 69
Domino, Fats, 37
Doucet, Michael, 8
Duke, David, 29

Edwards, Jay, 104
English language: Alafair's learning of, 20; and assimilation of Cajun people, 21, 25; Burke's interspersing standard English with other dialects, 14, 18, 22–23; dialect as regional variation of, 13; Robicheaux on importance of standard English, 20, 33; Robicheaux's use of, 25; and zydeco, 41
ethnic groups, 31, 36
étouffée, 58, 59, 63, 138n6

fais-do-dos (dances), 15, 44, 119
Faulkner, William, 120, 139n1
Festival of American Folklife, Washington DC, 56
feu follet (will-of-the-wisp), 77
filé, 57
film, 8–9, 10, 115–16
Fitzgerald, F. Scott, 61
floods and floodwaters, 6, 7
Florida, 59, 116
folk beliefs: in Burke's novels, 11–12, 65–66, 67, 71, 72, 73, 74–76, 77, 99–100; defining, 65–66. *See also* belief systems
folk groups, 18
folk justice: in Acadiana, 104–5; in Montana, 131; and Robicheaux's attitude toward violence, 103, 104, 105, 106, 109, 111
folk sayings: Aldous's use of, 13, 14, 25, 26–28, 31, 33, 135; Annie's understanding of, 14; Batist Perry's use of, 13–14, 26, 28–29, 33; and Burke's presentation of sense of place, 17, 33, 34, 135; and insider/outsider status, 17–18, 28; and Robicheaux's intimacy with readers, 26; Robicheaux's knowledge of, 13, 14; and Robicheaux's links to family roots, 17, 25–28, 31, 33; and Robicheaux's relationship with Alafair, 27; and Robicheaux's relationship with Batist, 28–29, 30; and Robicheaux's relationship with Bootsie, 29; as strategy to express politically incorrect feelings, 29–30; weather as basis for, 27
folk speech, 17–18
Fontenot, Canray, 41
food: as marker of ethnic identity, 55, 56, 138n2. *See also* Cajun foodways
French language: Batist Perry's use of, 19; Burke interspersing English language with, 14, 18, 22–23; Burke's transla-

tion and nontranslation of, 21, 24, 43; Burke's use of, 12–13, 14, 17–18, 20, 21, 24, 25; Cajun people identifying with, 20, 21, 25–26; Robicheaux's memories of people speaking, 120; Robicheaux's use of, 19, 25; sentence structure of, 21–22, 24–25, 28; and zydeco, 43. *See also* Cajun French; Creole French
French music, 36

Gaines, Ernest, 2
gangster language, 25
Gaudet, Marcia, 43
Gautreaux, Tim, 9, 57, 101, 108
gender roles: and food preparation methods, 60; and Robicheaux's attitude toward violence, 106–7
German immigrants, 36
ghosts: and belief systems, 65, 66, 77; in New Iberia, 6; and Robicheaux's encounters with Confederate soldiers, 7, 15, 79. *See also* revenants (returners, spirits of deceased)
Glass Rainbow, The (Burke): images of water in, 93; and Robicheaux's supernatural experiences, 79; as trilogy, 131
"Goodnight Irene" (song), 50
gratons, 62, 63
gris-gris, 70, 71, 73, 74–75
Guitar Slim, 46–47
Gulf of Mexico, 92, 93–95, 96, 97
gumbo, 55, 56–57, 59, 61–62, 63
Gutierrez, C. Paige, 138n1

Harrelson, Woody, 128
Hatfield-McCoy feud, 102
Heaven's Prisoners (Burke): Annie's murder in, 24, 28, 103–4, 105, 119; Batist Perry's dialect in, 20, 22–24; belief systems in, 75; Cajun foodways in, 58, 63; dialect in, 22–23; French language in, 24; folk sayings in, 27–28; "La Jolie Blonde" in, 39; Key West food in, 59; miscommunication in, 23; and Robicheaux's attitude toward violence, 103, 107; Robicheaux's description of New Iberia in, 119, 120–21; and Robicheaux's memories of Aldous, 119–21; Robicheaux's use of French language in, 20; as trilogy, 131
"Hey 'Tite Fille" (song), 44
Hill, Darlene Reimers, 62–63, 138n7
Hillerman, Tony, 3–4, 17, 18, 66–67, 133
Hispanic culture, 70–71
Holliday, Billie, 49
Honko, Lauri, 78, 138n1
Hood, John Bell, 86, 87–88, 89, 90, 91, 106–7
Hufford, David, 138n1
Hurricane Audrey, 7, 93–94
Hurricane Katrina, 7, 120, 122
Hurricane Rita, 122

Iberia Parish, 104, 105–6
International Rice Festival, 57
In the Electric Mist with Confederate Dead (Burke): Alafair's kidnapping in, 87–88, 91, 110, 111, 112; and Alafair's supernatural experiences, 85–86, 89; and Aldous's pistol, 85; bar scene in, 43–44; Cajun foodways in, 61; folk sayings in, 29–30; and Robicheaux on violence toward women, 106–7; and Robicheaux's attitude toward violence, 110–12; and Robicheaux's relationship with Bootsie, 88, 90–91; and Robicheaux's supernatural experiences, 79, 80, 84–88, 90; and water imagery, 97–98

jambalaya, 55, 56–57, 59
jazz music, 37
Jeanerette, La., 123
Jefferson, Blind Lemon, 49
Jesus Christ, 90, 91–92, 139n5
"Jolie Blonde, La" (song): Cajun culture associated with, 45; Robicheaux's associations with, 11, 32, 35, 37–40, 43, 45, 47, 52–54, 135; spellings of song's title, 38–39; updated version of, 37
Jolie Blon's Bounce (Burke): blues music in, 46–47; Cajun music in, 45; murder of local teenage girl in, 7, 45–46; popular music in, 37; Robicheaux's de-

Jolie Blon's Bounce (continued)
scription of Louisiana in, 124–25; Robicheaux's description of New Iberia in, 128; and Robicheaux's supernatural experiences, 91–92; zydeco in, 45–46
juré, 41–42
"Just a Dream" (song), 53, 54
justice system: Robicheaux's lack of faith in, 106–7. *See also* folk justice

Kalčik, Susan, 138n2
Key West, Fla., 59
Kirshenblatt-Gimblett, Barbara, 127, 139n2

Lafayette, La., 57–58, 113–14, 115, 116, 120, 127
language: Batist Perry's use of, 13, 19; Burke's presentation of locale through, 12–13, 14, 17, 22–23, 33–34, 135; gangster language, 25; and insider/outsider status, 24, 28, 31; and moments of crisis, 24; Purcel's use of, 13; and Robicheaux's code switching, 23–24, 137n2; Robicheaux's use of, 1, 13–14. *See also* Cajun French; Creole French; dialects; English language; French language
Last Car to Elysian Fields (Burke): Batist Perry on music in, 50; blues music in, 49–52; folk sayings in, 31; intermingling of fictional and historical characters in, 49–50
Leadbelly (Huddie Ledbetter), 49–50
Ledbetter, Sarie, 49
LeJeune, Iry, 38
Lewis, Jerry Lee, 48
Lewis, Smiley, 47
Light of the World (Burke): Montana as setting of, 118, 129–30, 131; Purcel in, 118, 129–30, 132; Robicheaux's description of New Iberia in, 130; Robicheaux's relationship with Alafair in, 129–30; water imagery in, 98–99, 130
local place names, pronunciation of, 18
Lomax, Alan, 41–42, 49, 50
Lomax, John, 49, 50

Longfellow, Henry Wadsworth, *Evangeline*, 9
Louisiana: death penalty in, 104; dialects identifying different groups in, 18–19; foodways used in promoting, 10–11; oil industry in, 5, 14, 37, 60, 79, 93, 97, 101, 103, 114, 120, 122–23, 125; popularity of Cajun music in, 35; Robicheaux's description of, 123, 124–25; as setting for Burke's novels, 1, 4; as setting for detective novels, 4; water environment of, 92, 98–99. *See also* Acadiana; *and specific cities*
loup-garou (werewolf), 23, 65, 77

McConaughey, Matthew, 128
Mardi Gras, 4
Mason, Bobbie Ann, 62–63
memorates, 78
Milton, John, 131
Mississippi, 8
"Mo Cher Cousin" (song), 43
Montana: Burke's residence in, 8, 116, 118, 129; Burke's use as setting in novels, 118, 129–30, 131; folk justice in, 131; Robicheaux's visits to, 8, 20, 98–99, 116, 118, 136
Montell, William Lynwood, 104, 107–8, 109, 139n3
Morning for Flamingos, A (Burke): belief systems in, 70, 72, 74; and responsibility for Annie's murder, 106; Robicheaux's restraint from violence in, 106; and Robicheaux's supernatural experiences, 97; zydeco in, 42–43
Mulate's, Breaux Bridge, 11, 61, 62, 126

National Trust for Historic Preservation, 127
Native Americans: Cajun foodways incorporating traditions of, 57, 138n3; Cajun music incorporating traditions of, 36; and folk beliefs, 73; folk sayings of, 30; foodways of, 56
Navajo culture, 3–4, 17, 18, 66, 133
Nazis, 7

Index

NCIS: New Orleans (television show), 4
Neon Rain, The (Burke): Aldous's communication with Robicheaux in, 80; belief systems in, 74–75; blues in, 48; Cajun foodways in, 59, 60; cultural roots established in, 21; dialect in, 21–22; folk sayings in, 26–27; New Orleans as setting of, 5–6, 8, 59; Robicheaux introduced and established in, 1, 26–27, 116; Robicheaux's attitude toward violence in, 108; Robicheaux's memories of Aldous in, 120; Robicheaux's memories of New Iberia in, 120; and Robicheaux's supernatural experiences, 80; Robicheaux's violence in, 106, 109; as trilogy, 131
New Iberia, La.: Burke's childhood in, 6–7, 114, 128; Burke's creation of identity for, 113, 114, 115, 116, 118–19, 127, 128, 135; and Burke's use of local events, 7; and Cajun foodways, 60; as cultural tourism destination, 3, 15, 116, 126–28, 129, 139n2; Lafayette compared to, 113–14; New Orleans compared to, 5–6, 59, 113, 117, 120; Robicheaux identified with, 8, 14–15, 113, 117, 118, 119, 126–27, 128, 131–32, 133, 135–36; Robicheaux's descriptions of, 116–17, 119, 120–21, 124, 128, 129, 130, 134; Robicheaux's descriptions of race relations in, 123–24; Robicheaux's memories of boyhood home, 8, 39, 40, 113, 119–21, 123; as setting for Burke's novels, 1, 4, 5–6, 7, 8, 14–16, 113, 128–29
New Orleans, La.: Catholicism in, 72; culture of, 115, 130–31, 133; festivals of, 57–58; food of, 59, 62; gangster language of, 25; jazz music of, 37; Mafia in, 122; New Iberia compared to, 5–6, 59, 113, 117, 120; portions of Robicheaux stories in, 5–6, 8, 59, 113, 116, 117, 130; Robicheaux's description of, 124; Robicheaux's description of dialect in, 130; as setting in detective novels, 4, 5, 133; violence in, 110, 118; voodoo associated with, 67, 69–72
New South, 117
New Testament, 90, 91–92, 139n5
No Mercy (film), 8, 115

okra, 61
Orbison, Roy, 48

Parker, Robert B., 3, 114, 133
Passion Fish (film), 8
past: Burke informing novels with sense of, 102; Burke's portrayal of Robicheaux's past, 6, 11; Burke's portrayal of past and present intertwined, 36, 88, 89, 97, 100, 120, 128–29, 136; Robicheaux's connection with, through food, 56; Robicheaux's connection with, through music, 11, 35, 37–40, 44, 46–47, 52–54; Robicheaux's internal conflict stemming from fondness for, 6, 125; Robicheaux's memories of, 38–39, 44, 52, 93–96, 120, 128; Robicheaux's preoccupation with, 37, 77, 88–89, 126, 129; and Robicheaux's supernatural experiences, 78, 79, 83, 85–89, 92; Robicheaux's use of Cajun French, 18, 30–32, 33; and water imagery, 93–94, 95, 97
Pegasus Descending (Burke), 30–31
Perkins, Carl, 48
Pitre, Glen, 104
poboys, 59
Presley, Elvis, 48
Price, Lloyd, 47
Prudhomme, Paul, 8, 15, 57, 59, 115
Purple Cane Road (Burke): blues music in, 47; folk sayings in, 29; Purcel's and Batist Perry's perception of red moon in, 29, 30; water imagery in, 93–94

race and race relations: Batist Perry's attitudes toward, 30, 31, 50; in Breaux Bridge, 61–62; Burke on racial distinctions, 31, 52; and Cajun music, 36, 40–41, 45; and folk sayings, 29–30; in

151

Index

race and race relations (*continued*)
New Iberia, 6, 114; Robicheaux's description of, 123–24; and zydeco, 45
Rayne Frog Festival, 57
redfish industry, 59, 138n4
Reed, John Shelton, 102, 105, 139n2, 139n3
religion: Robicheaux's attitudes toward, 11–12; slave religion, 67, 72; water as element of religious faith, 12, 93. *See also* belief systems; Catholicism; New Testament
revenants (returners, spirits of deceased): Aldous as revenant, 25, 26–27, 79, 80–81, 83, 95–96, 100, 134, 136; Annie as revenant, 12, 79, 80–84, 91, 93, 97, 99, 134; Burke's view of function of, 79, 80, 139n2; and Burke's view of water, 92, 99; purpose of, 78–79, 80, 82, 84, 87, 88, 89, 90, 91, 92; and Robicheaux's crisis periods, 12, 79, 82, 83, 84, 91, 92; Robicheaux's experiences of, 79, 80–90, 91, 92, 99; types of, 78, 79
rhythm & blues music, 46
rice, 56, 57, 58
roux, 57, 58, 61–62, 138n5, 138n6

sauce piquante, 57, 59, 138n6
Savannah, Ga., 126
Savoy, Marc, 36
sense of place: and Burke's development of Robicheaux's character, 133–36; and Burke's use of Cajun culture, 3, 17, 134, 136; and Burke's use of Cajun foodways, 61–62, 63, 64, 135, 138n7; and Burke's use of folk beliefs, 73; and Burke's use of folk sayings, 17, 33, 34, 135; and Burke's use of language, 12–13, 14, 17, 22–23, 33–34, 135; and Burke's use of music, 54, 135
slavery: and folk sayings as survival strategies, 30; folk songs from, 43; and slave religion, 67, 72; and violence, 106–7
Smith, Julie, 4–5, 113, 133
Smith, Lee, 107–8
social class, Robicheaux's description of, 123–24

soul music, 46
South: foodways of, 62–63, 64; jails of, 70; myths of, 117; Robicheaux's description of, 121–22; and southern fiction genre, 3, 102, 110, 112, 139n2; violence of, 101, 102–4, 107–8, 109, 110–11, 112, 139n2, 139n3
Southern Comfort (film), 8, 115–16
Stained White Radiance, A (Burke): Batist Perry's folk sayings in, 28–29; Bootsie's illness in, 68; Cajun foodways in, 58; folk sayings in, 28–29; "La Jolie Blonde" in, 39–40; Robicheaux's belief systems in, 68; Robicheaux's description of Atchafalaya Basin in, 117–18; Robicheaux's description of New Iberia in, 116–17, 121, 129; and traiteurs, 73; and zydeco, 40
storytelling: Aldous as storyteller, 25, 26, 33; French language as identity marker in, 21, 25–26
Sunset Limited (Burke), 19
swamp pop: Bernard on, 37, 137n1; role in Burke's novels, 36, 37, 52–53

Texas, 8, 41
"Things That I Used to Do, The" (song), 46–47
time: nature of, 79, 83, 88–89, 92. *See also* past
Toups, Wayne, 35
tourism: and Cajun foodways, 58, 61, 62; and Cajun music, 40; of New Iberia, 3, 15, 116, 126–28, 129, 139n2
traiteurs (traditional healers): Burke's use of, 12, 67–68, 72, 75, 76, 77; and local custom, 23; negative connotations associated with, 72, 75; Robicheaux's encounters with, 42–43, 68, 70, 71; and variety of coexisting belief systems, 12, 66, 72, 76, 77
True Detective (HBO series), 127–28
two-step (dance), 44–45

Victor's Cafeteria, New Iberia, 126, 129
Vietnam War: Robicheaux as veteran of, 2, 3, 9; and Robicheaux's attitude

Index

toward violent acts, 101, 109; Robicheaux's injuries from, 9; and Robicheaux's malaria, 90; and Robicheaux's supernatural experiences, 79, 81, 84, 89, 91–92, 98
violence: of Aldous, 101, 103, 108, 120; of Batist Perry, 109–10; in Burke's novels, 101, 102, 109, 110, 112, 139n2; cultural norms of, 103–4, 106, 107–8, 109, 110–11; ordinary people's lives touched by, 22; Purcel's views of, 101, 110; Robicheaux as violent man, 10, 101; and Robicheaux's defense or protection of someone, 103, 109–10, 111, 112; and Robicheaux's fights, 24; and Robicheaux's reaction to personal matters, 102–3, 104, 107, 111; and slavery, 106–7; of South, 101, 102–4, 107–8, 109, 110–11, 112, 139n2, 139n3; and water imagery, 94
von Sydow, Carl W., 78, 138n1
voodoo: in Burke's novels, 67, 69–70, 73, 77; and folk beliefs, 65, 66, 67, 71–72; and traiteurs, 67, 70, 71, 72

water: and Aldous's death, 93, 94–97, 99; as element of religious faiths, 12, 93; floods and floodwaters, 6, 7; as giving and taking life, 89, 93–97, 98; liminal quality of, 92–93; as link between living and dead, 12, 99; and Robicheaux's certainty that the dead inhabit the rain, 83, 98, 99; and Robicheaux's relationship with Alafair, 93, 95, 97; and Robicheaux's supernatural experiences, 12, 77–78, 81, 83, 85, 92, 96–99, 134
weather patterns: as basis for folk sayings, 27; in Burke's novels, 7; Robicheaux's memories of, 98–99
western swing music, 41
Williams, John, 128
Wilson, Justin, 57, 115
Wiltz, Chris, 4–5, 59, 113, 130–31, 133, 138n4
wisdom, of folk sayings, 14, 25–26, 28, 33
World War II, 21

Zuñi culture, 66
Zydecajun, 35
zydeco: African Americans claiming, 36, 42; and Cajun foodways, 61; and Cajun music, 40–41, 45; and English language, 41; and juré, 41–42; Robicheaux's reaction to, 42, 44; role in Burke's novels, 36, 42–43, 44; style of dance associated with, 44, 45